THE SABERMETRIC REVOLUTION

THE SABERMETRIC REVOLUTION

ASSESSING THE GROWTH OF ANALYTICS IN BASEBALL

BENJAMIN BAUMER
AND
ANDREW ZIMBALIST

PENN

UNIVERSITY OF PENNSYLVANIA PRESS

PHILADELPHIA

Published by
University of Pennsylvania Press
Philadelphia, Pennsylvania 19104-4112
www.upenn.edu/pennpress

Printed in the United States of America
on acid-free paper

2 4 6 8 10 9 7 5 3 1

Library of Congress Cataloging-in-Publication Data
Baumer, Benjamin.
    The sabermetric revolution : assessing the growth of analytics in baseball / Benjamin
Baumer and Andrew Zimbalist. — 1st ed.
        p. cm.
    Includes bibliographical references and index.
    ISBN 978-0-8122-4572-1 (hardcover : alk. paper)
    1. Baseball—Statistical methods. 2. Baseball—Mathematical models. I. Zimbalist,
Andrew S. II. Title.
    GV877.B38 2014
    796.357021—dc23
                                                              2013026520

For all the left arms that made it,
and all those that didn't

CONTENTS

PREFACE

_____

Michael Lewis wrote *Moneyball* because he fell in love with a story. The story is about how intelligent innovation (the creative use of statistical analysis) in the face of market inefficiency (the failure of all other teams to use available information productively) can overcome the unfairness of baseball economics (rich teams can buy all the best players) to enable a poor team to slay the giants. Lewis is an engaging storyteller and, along the way, introduces us to intriguing characters who carry forward the rags-to-riches plot. By the end, the story of the 2002 Oakland A's and their general manager, Billy Beane, is so well told that we believe its portrayal of baseball history, economics, and competitive success. The result is a new Horatio Alger tale that reinforces a beloved American myth and, all the better, applies to our national pastime.

The appeal of Lewis's *Moneyball* was sufficiently strong that Hollywood wanted a piece of the action. With a compelling script, smart direction, and the handsome Brad Pitt as Beane, *Moneyball* became part of mass culture and its perceived validity—and its legend—only grew.

This book will attempt to set the record straight on *Moneyball* and the role of "analytics" in baseball. Whether one believes Lewis's account or not, it had a significant impact on baseball management. Following the book's publication in 2003, team after team began to create their own analytics or sabermetric sub-departments within baseball operations. Today, over three-quarters of major league teams have individuals dedicated to performing these functions. Many teams have multiple staffers creatively parsing numbers.

In a world where the average baseball team payroll exceeds $100 million and the average team generates $250 million in revenue each year, the hiring of one, two, or three sabermetricians, at salaries ranging from $30,000 to $125,000, can practically be an afterthought. (Sabermetricians is what Bill

James called individuals who statistically analyze baseball performance, named after the Society for American Baseball Research, SABR.) Particularly, once the expectation of prospective insight and gain is in place and other teams join the movement, a team that does not hire a sabermetrician could be accused of malpractice. In baseball, much like the rest of the world, executives and managers are subject to loss aversion. Many of their actions are motivated not by which decision or investment offers the highest potential return, but by which decision will insulate them best from criticism for neglecting to follow the conventional wisdom. So, to some degree, the sabermetric wildfire in baseball is a product of group behavior or conformism.

Meanwhile, the proliferation of data on baseball performance and its extensive accessibility, as well as the emergence of myriad statistical services and practitioner websites, have imbued sabermetrics with the quality of a fad. The fact that it is a fad, much like rotisserie baseball leagues, fantasy football leagues, and video games, does not mean that it doesn't contain some underlying validity and value. One of our tasks in this book will be to decipher what parts of baseball analytics are faddish and what parts are meritorious.

Some of the new metrics, such as the one that purports to assess fielding ability accurately (UZR), are black boxes, wherein the authors hold their method to be proprietary and will not reveal how they are calculated. The problem is that this makes the metric's value much more difficult to evaluate. Of course, fads, like myths, are more easily perpetuated when it is not possible to shed light on their inner workings.

Here are some questions that need to be answered. What is the state of knowledge and insight that emanates from sabermetric research? How has it influenced the competitive success of teams? Does the incorporation of sabermetric insight into player evaluation and on-the-field strategy help to overcome the financial disadvantage of small market teams and, thereby, promote competitive balance in the game? Lewis's account in *Moneyball* exudes optimism on all counts.

Beyond the rags-to-riches theme, Lewis's story echoes another well-worn refrain in modern culture—the perception that quantification is scientific. Given that our world is increasingly dominated by the TV, the computer, the tablet, and the smartphone—all forms of electronic communication and dependent on binary signaling—it is perhaps understandable that society genuflects before numbers and statistics. Yet the fetish of quantification well predates modern electronic communications.

Consider, for instance, the school of industrial management that was spawned by Frederick Winslow Taylor over a hundred years ago. Taylor argued that it was possible to improve worker productivity through a process that scientifically evaluated each job. This evaluation entailed, among other components, the measurement of each worker's physical movements in the production process and use of a stopwatch to assess the optimal length of time it should take to perform each movement. On this basis, an optimal output expectation could be set for each worker and the worker's pay could be linked, via a piece rate system, to the worker's output.[1] The Taylorist system was known as "scientific management" and was promulgated widely during the first decades of the twentieth century. The purported benefits of scientific management, however, proved to be spurious and the school was supplanted by another—one that emphasized the human relations of production. Thus, obsession with quantification at the expense of human relations met with failure.[2]

Baseball, much more than other team sports, lends itself to measurement. The game unfolds in a restricted number of discrete plays and outcomes. When an inning begins, there are no outs and no one is on base. After one batter, there is either one out or no outs and a runner on first, second or third base, or no outs and a run will have scored. In fact, at any point in time during a game, there are twenty-four possible discrete situations. There are eight possible combinations of base runners: (1) no one on base; (2) a runner on first; (3) a runner on second; (4) a runner on third; (5) runners on first and second; (6) runners on first and third; (7) runners on second and third; (8) runners on first, second, and third. For each of these combinations of base runners, there can be either zero, one, or two outs. Eight runner alignments and three different out situations makes twenty-four discrete situations. (It is on this grid of possible situations that the run expectancy matrix, to be discussed in later chapters, is based.)

Compare that to basketball. There are virtually an infinite number of positions on the floor where the five offensive players can be standing (or moving across). Five different players can be handling the ball.

Or, compare it to football. Each team has four downs to go ten yards. The offensive series can begin at any yard line (or half- or quarter-yard line) on the field. The eleven offensive players can align themselves in a myriad of possible formations; likewise the defense. After one play, it can be second and ten yards to go, or second and nine and a half, or second and three, or second and twelve, and so on.

Moreover, in baseball, performance is much less interdependent than it is in other team sports. A batter gets a hit, or a pitcher records a strikeout, largely on his own. He does not need a teammate to throw a precise pass or make a decisive block. If a batter in baseball gets on base 40 percent of the time and hits 30 home runs, he is going to be one of the leading batters in the game. If a quarterback completes 55 percent of his passes, though, to assess his prowess we also to need to know something about his offensive line and his receivers.

So, while the measurement of a player's performance is possible in all sports, its potential for more complete and accurate description is greater in baseball. It is, therefore, not surprising that since its early days, baseball has produced a copious quantitative record. Although one might not know it from either the book or the movie *Moneyball*, the keeping of complex records and the analytical processing of these records reaches back at least several decades prior to the machinations of Billy Beane and the Oakland A's at the beginning of the twenty-first century.

Our book proceeds as follows. To clarify some matters of artistic license presented as fact, Chapter 1 discusses the book and the movie *Moneyball*, what they get right, what they get wrong and various sins of omission. Chapter 2 traces the growing presence of statistical analysis in baseball front offices. Chapters 3 and 4 introduce and survey the current state of sabermetric knowledge for offense and defense, respectively. Chapter 5 sketches the *Moneyball* diaspora, that is, the growing application of statistical analysis to understand performance and strategy in other sports, principally basketball and football. Chapter 6 illustrates the use of statistical analysis to penetrate the business of baseball, particularly its effects on competitive balance. Chapter 7 assesses sabermetrics' success, or lack thereof, in improving team performance.

Finally, it is useful to clarify some vocabulary before proceeding. *Sabermetrics* means the use of statistical methods to analyze player performance and game strategy. *Baseball analytics* also means the use of statistical methods to assess player performance and game strategy, but it further involves the use of statistical methods to evaluate team and league business decisions. The term *analytics* as applied to sports has also come to include the interpretation of digital video images, often with associated quantity metrics. We use *moneyball* (with the lowercase *m*) to mean the application of sabermetrics with the goal of identifying player skills and players that the market undervalues.

1

Revisiting *Moneyball*

Michael Lewis's 2003 bestselling book *Moneyball* has sold well over a million copies. The 2011 movie *Moneyball* has exceeded $120 million in box-office sales and was nominated for six Academy Awards, including best actor and best picture. It is safe to assume that the story that Michael Lewis fell in love with back in 2002 has been widely assimilated by people who care about baseball as well as by many who don't. The book was a significant catalyst in spreading the sabermetric gospel in baseball front offices, as well as feeding the growing popularity of sports analytics over the Internet, in academia, and in fantasy sports leagues. In a sense, the book brought into the mainstream the incorporation of sabermetric practice within the baseball industry, much as Bill James had popularized new statistical ways of understanding the game and its players.

Yet, for all its storytelling virtues, the book, though containing an underlying truth, substantially misrepresents baseball reality, and the 2011 movie, as movies are wont to do, distorts reality still further. Thus, before we begin our discussion of the intellectual state of baseball analytics, its application in the industry, and its future prospects, it is important to clear away the popular debris that has been left behind by the two versions of *Moneyball*.

Moneyball on Screen

The film has the same basic storyline, stripped of its emotional embellishments and flourishes, as the million-copy-selling book. The Oakland A's, a small market team with a parsimonious owner, needed to find a way to remain competitive after the 2001 season. The team was going to lose three of its star players (Jason Giambi, Johnny Damon, and Jason Isringhausen) to free agency (and to the Yankees, Red Sox, and Cardinals, respectively), and the owner would not provide the cash to sign any worthy replacements. The A's general manager (GM), Billy Beane, travels to Cleveland to discuss a trade for relief pitcher Ricardo Rincon and discovers that Cleveland GM Mark Shapiro is paying close attention to the opinions of a dorky-looking Yale grad on his staff (called Peter Brand on screen). After the meeting, Beane corners Brand in the parking lot and presses him to reveal how he approaches valuing baseball players. An enthralled Beane hires Brand and adopts a unique strategy to assemble a winning team based on Brand's philosophy. (Brand's character was based on the real-life Paul DePodesta, a tall, slender Harvard grad. Once he saw what the screenplay did with his character, DePodesta did not give permission to have his name used for the film.)

A central tenet of this unconventional philosophy is that teams pay too much attention to a hitter's batting average (BA) and not enough attention to a player's on-base percentage (OBP, roughly batting average plus walk rate and hit by pitch rate). The basic idea is that walks were dramatically undervalued; just like a hit, a walk puts a runner on base, avoids an out, and brings another batter up to the plate. Of course, many have also observed that players with a good eye at the plate help to run up the pitch count of the starting pitcher and accelerate getting into the opposing team's bullpen.

In the movie, Peter Brand's approach, in turn, is represented as being derived from that of Bill James. By focusing on OBP, the A's could identify undervalued players and assemble a winning team on the cheap. (This is the idea of a market inefficiency. The actors in the market are making decisions based on incomplete or wrong information which means that some inputs—players in this case—are systematically paid more and others less than they are worth.)

The movie and the book both make the case that the A's implemented this philosophy. Further, it is represented that the strategy worked and explains why the team won an American League record twenty straight games and the AL Western Division title in 2002.

One of the most dramatic events in the movie occurs when Billy Beane walks into the team clubhouse after a loss and sees the players dancing to music, led by outfielder Jeremy Giambi. (Beane acquired Giambi via trade before the 2000 season, but he is represented as having been acquired by the A's during 2001–2002 offseason due to his high OBP and in order to help replace the lost OBP from his brother Jason.) The next morning Beane arrives at his office and, against the advice of his guru Peter Brand, in a fit makes two trades: sending Jeremy Giambi to Philadelphia for John Mabry and trading the A's first baseman Carlos Peña to the Detroit Tigers for cash. Peña was reputed to be a leading candidate for Rookie of the Year honors, but A's manager Art Howe was playing him instead of Scott Hatteberg, whom both Beane and Brand had designated as their first baseman. Jeremy Giambi, at the time of the trade, had an impressive OBP of .390, which only rose further, to .435, after he went to the Phillies. Meanwhile, John Mabry had a below-average OBP of .304 at the time of the trade and a subpar OBP of .322 with the A's. (The average OBP in major league baseball hovers around .333, with small variance from year to year.) Mabry had only been weaker in earlier years, with an OBP below .300 in 1999, 2000, and 2001. Why would Beane make this trade?

After the trades, according to the screenplay, the mood in the clubhouse changes and the A's suddenly become a winning team. The Giambi trade is shown as occurring on May 22, and the turnaround takes place after the team's loss to the Orioles, 11 to 3, on May 23. The A's record was 20 wins and 26 losses at this point. Following the loss on May 23, the A's won five consecutive games and 24 of their next 29. By June 24, the A's record was 44 and 31.

While it isn't elaborated, the viewer is led to believe that the substitution of Hatteberg for Peña at first base was a key element to the team's newfound success. One of the problems with this presentation is that Peña was not, in fact, traded until six weeks later, on July 5. Thus, the whole notion that the trades of Giambi and Peña were (a) based on sabermetric principles and (b) responsible for the team's turnaround is belied by the facts.

Of lesser significance, a few other matters of artistic license in the film should be mentioned. First, the A's frugal owner, Steve Schott, actually bought the team from the estate of Walter Haas in 1995 and had been enforcing a tight budget from the beginning. The imperative to build a winning team on a shoestring budget did not begin in 2002. Second, no GM, and certainly not one on a tight budget, would fly across the country to discuss a potential trade for a relief pitcher, and when GMs discuss trades they don't do so with eight other people in the room (possibly excepting a rare occasion at baseball's winter meetings). The meeting was dreamed up as a way to introduce Paul DePodesta (aka Peter Brand) into the story. After the meeting Beane calls Brand and tells him that he's been "bought" by the A's. In fact, what happened is that in November 1998 (fully three years earlier) the A's asked the Indians for permission to make DePodesta (Brand) their assistant general manager and the Indians agreed. Third, at the time of the apocryphal meeting, Mark Shapiro was not GM of the Indians, as shown in the movie.

Fourth, there are various sins of omission, but perhaps the most glaring is that Sandy Alderson is left out of the film altogether. Alderson served as GM of the Oakland A's from 1983 through 1997. He hired Billy Beane and made him his assistant GM in 1993. More important, it was Alderson who introduced sabermetrics into the A's organization in the mid-1980s (more on this below) and to Beane in the mid-1990s. Alderson was in the film's early script, but his character was excised before the final version.

Fifth, there is, of course, the use of hyperbole throughout for cinematic effect.[1] Listen to Paul DePodesta reflect on the film and describe the actual relationship between the stats analysts and the traditional scouts in the A's clubhouse: "I think it's overblown. . . . Surely there were spirited debates at different times internally, but they were always very respectful, with everybody largely on the same page. . . . Even some of the metrics we came up with were things that were born out of conversations we had with longtime scouts. So it really was an organization which I think was bound together much more than has been portrayed."[2]

Sixth, Billy Beane, in a heated exchange with Art Howe, asserts that "I don't care about righty/lefty."[3] Yet, if Beane were a true student of sabermetrics, he would know that there is ample evidence, going back at least to the statistical work of George Lindsey in the 1950s, that platooning can have a substantial effect on hitting success. (Lindsey, based on a statistical analysis of 400 games from the 1950s, found facing a pitcher of the opposite hand raised batting averages by a mean of 32 points.)[4]

Seventh, Beane quips to the A's players, "No more stealing." This is a bastardization of the sabermetric wisdom. Although different analysts come to slightly different estimates, the basic sabermetric conclusion is that in an average game situation, a runner should only attempt to steal second base if he has at least a 65 percent chance of success.[5] Runners with a lower success percentage reduce the expected number of runs scored in an inning by attempting base thievery. This inference, of course, also varies by the game situation, the pitcher's move to first, speed of delivery, and pitch velocity, the catcher's release and arm strength, among other factors. Further, the sabermetric wisdom is itself limited by an inadequate consideration of how the threat of a steal affects the pitcher's concentration, selection of pitches, and stamina. The notion that a saber-savvy GM would outlaw base stealing is, at best, misguided.

We discuss baserunning at greater length in subsequent chapters, but it is interesting here to note that the A's seem to have shifted strategy on stolen bases in recent years. During the twenty-two-year period from 1990 through 2011, the average major league team attempted 147.5 stolen bases per season. During the early moneyball years, 2002–2007, the A's attempted only 66 stolen bases on average; yet during the three-year period 2009–2011, the A's were well above the long-term MLB average with 178 stolen base attempts per year. However, considering the five years since 2007, the A's average attempts were just below the MLB average at 142 per year.[6] What these variations suggest is that stolen bases vary as much according to team personnel as to team strategy. One reason why the A's have attempted more stolen bases since 2007 is that they have more effective base stealers on their roster: the team's average stolen base success rate jumped from 70.3 percent during 2003–2007 to 76.9 percent during 2007–2011. (The major league average success rate since 1990 is 69.3 percent.)

Eighth, one of the movie's more dramatic moments is at the end when Beane flies to Boston to meet with Red Sox owner John Henry at Fenway Park. Beane receives a job offer on a piece of paper from Henry. We are later informed that the offer was for $12.5 million. In the movie, Beane decides not to take the offer. In real life, Beane flew from the owners' meeting in Arizona to meet John Henry at Henry's winter home in Boca Raton, Florida.

Beane returned to the meetings and then flew home to Oakland to contemplate Henry's offer (which was for $2.5 million annually over five years). The next day Beane called Henry and accepted. Champagne bottles were popped open on both ends of the call. The only issue remaining was agreeing on the compensation to the A's from the Red Sox for the prospective loss of Beane. Henry waited for a call the next day from Beane to finalize the compensation. No call came and Henry tried in vain to reach Beane. Finally, Henry called Steve Schott (the A's owner), who told Henry that he didn't think that Beane was going to go to Boston. Later in the day Beane finally called Henry and confirmed that he was staying in Oakland.

Other than these minor misleading elements, the movie, albeit with some simplification and some added familial drama, is faithful to the book. However, both suffer from a fundamental misrepresentation of what happened in Oakland and its relationship to the principles of moneyball.

The Book

Lewis's central argument is that the A's, through the systematic application of new statistical analysis, were able to produce a winning team despite being from a small market and having an undersized budget. A collateral argument is that the underlying analysis was derived from the work of Bill James and that the broad use of the analytic techniques to evaluate players' performance and game strategy was new to baseball. We will argue that the "new" Jamesian metrics, while not new in either conception or application, are indeed important, but they do not fully explain the A's on-field success during the early years of the 2000s. That said, the A's were an industry leader in adopting new metrics and identifying market inefficiencies, and some part of their strong performance under Billy Beane may be related to these factors. We will discuss the evidence of the A's overall approach to player development and strategy in Chapter 7; presently, we will focus on the 2002 season, as does *Moneyball*.

The 2002 Season

In 2002, the A's finished in first place in their division, winning over one hundred games, but were eliminated in the first round of the playoffs. Lewis describes the team's success that season as well as the A's strategy and analysis in preparing for the 2002 amateur draft. We discuss each in turn.

Although Lewis mentions in passing the contributions of A's shortstop Miguel Tejada, third baseman Eric Chavez, and pitchers Barry Zito, Mark Mulder, and Tim Hudson, his principal and overriding contention is that the A's success was tied to the incorporation of sabermetric insights. Yet Billy Beane's player moves during 2002 did not build upon what was probably the most prominent sabermetric measure at the time, and the one emphasized by Lewis—OBP. Trading away Jeremy Giambi and Carlos Peña and getting back only John Mabry actually provided a net loss of OBP. The acquisition of David Justice and the team's other minor moves did not compensate for this, so that the A's OBP in 2002 was .339, compared to .345 in 2001 and .360 in 2000.[7] If anything, the team seemed to be moving in a counter-sabermetric direction in 2002, at least based on the OBP metric emphasized by Lewis.

An alternative explanation of the A's 2002 success seems far more persuasive. The A's had two of the strongest hitters in the American League: 2002 league MVP Miguel Tejada and Gold Glove–winning third baseman Eric Chavez. Tejada and Chavez each had 34 home runs, 131 and 109 RBI, and .861 and .860 OPS (a measure of offensive performance combining OBP with slugging), respectively. Both Chavez and Tejada are referred to in the book as "Mr. Swing at Everything," meaning that neither one was patient at the plate and neither followed the fundamental sabermetric tenet of working a walk.[8]

One of the most complex and inclusive measures of player performance is WAR (wins above replacement player), which we will discuss in Chapter 4.[9] Tejada and Chavez had a combined WAR of 9.2. Between them, they accounted for 41 percent of the team's total WAR from its position players.[10]

The A's also had three of the top ten pitchers in the American League that year. One of them, Barry Zito, won the Cy Young Award. Barry Zito's WAR was 6.9, Tim Hudson's was 6.6, and Mark Mulder's was 4.4, making the combined WAR of these top three pitchers 17.9 out of 25.3 for the entire pitching staff. Nearly all of the remaining WAR for the staff was accumulated by three pitchers: fourth starter Cory Lidle (3.3), closer Billy Koch (1.7), and right-handed submariner Chad Bradford (1.5). No other pitcher's WAR was statistically distinguishable from zero.[11] Yet while Bradford received extended treatment (an exclusive, full chapter) by Michael Lewis, the other five were mentioned only in passing, despite accounting for 90.5 percent of the total WAR of the pitching staff. The selection of these five pitchers was based on traditional scouting reports and performance measures.[12]

Bradford does have an interesting story and a unique delivery, but as we saw above, his contribution to the A's success in 2002 was relatively minor. Lewis goes through significant contortions to establish Bradford's bona fides. Thus, for example, he writes: "Dropping his release point had various effects, but the most obvious was to reduce the distance between his hand, when the ball left it, and the catcher's mitt. His 84-mile-per-hour fastball took about as much time to reach the plate as a more conventionally delivered 94-mile-per-hour one."[13] Sound implausible? It is. To increase from 84 mph to 94 mph is an 11.9 percent increase in speed. To achieve this, Bradford's hand would have to be 11.9 percent of 60 feet and 6 inches closer to home plate when he released the ball than a typical pitcher's hand. That is, Bradford's hand would have to be fully 7 feet and 2.4 inches closer to home plate than a typical pitcher's hand! Lewis attributes this closer proximity (equal to a bit more than Shaquille O'Neal's height) to the fact that Bradford throws underhand. It is not obvious why the angle of delivery should affect proximity to home plate.[14]

Last, consider the A's performance in various statistical categories relative to the league average in 2002. The A's OBP was 2.4 percent above the American League average and its OPS was 2.1 percent above. On the pitching side, the A's pitching staff's ERA+ was 18 percent above average, its strike out-to-walk ratio 12 percent above and its WHIP 7.7 percent above, all suggesting a stronger contribution from pitching than hitting to the A's success in 2002.[15] Of course, an appreciable part of the team's pitching performance was likely a product of the team's defense—another central aspect of success virtually ignored by Lewis.

The 2002 Amateur Draft

Lewis devotes well over a chapter to discussing the A's 2002 June amateur draft strategy and picks. Again, the underlying premise is that Beane employed saber-savvy analysis to discern the diamonds in the rough and outsmart his competition. Lewis characterizes the A's analysis of prospects prior to the 2002 draft as a collaborative process. But, says Lewis, the 2001 draft had been a disaster, and in 2002 Beane decided that he would remove the scouts and their conventional "tools"-based evaluation from the process, and rely entirely on his statistical analysis.[16]

Although Lewis sat in on some of the A's strategic draft discussions and he extols the wisdom behind the identification of the team's top choices, Lewis published *Moneyball* in 2003, prior to the maturation of the A's 2002 top picks. The 2002 draft promised to be a fruitful one for the A's, who were in the unique and highly enviable position of having seven first-round picks. If Lewis's theory were correct, ten years later we should have witnessed the flowering of these young prospects. What is the record?

Using sabermetric principles, Beane and DePodesta identified eight pitchers and twelve position players whom they would draft in a perfect world, if money were no object. The A's signed thirteen of these twenty players, an unexpected coup that left Beane ecstatic. One of the A's seven first-round picks was catcher Jeremy Brown. Brown is singled out by Lewis as an especially enlightened choice by Beane; indeed, Chapter 5 is entitled "The Jeremy Brown Blue Plate Special." How did this enlightened pick turn out? Not so well. In his professional baseball career, Brown had a total of ten major league at bats.[17]

The A's third pick in the first round was a shortstop named John McCurdy. McCurdy never played a major league game. Of Oakland's remaining top thirteen picks in 2002, only Nick Swisher (the A's first pick) has had a clearly above-average major league career, and, as Lewis acknowledges, Swisher was a favorite of both Beane and the scouts. Of the other ten players, only three (Joe Blanton, Mark Teahen, and John Baker) have played significantly in the majors.[18] DePodesta thought that one of the seven players who never made it to the Show, Brant Colamarino, "might be the best hitter in the country."[19]

A fair accounting of the *Moneyball* draft, with the benefit of hindsight, reveals a mixed bag, rather than the coup that is depicted by Lewis. Using data from the sixteen amateur drafts during 1990–2005, we constructed two models for the expected return—in terms of WAR accumulated during a player's first six major league seasons—of any of the first 220 draft slots in each year.[20] In essence, the first thirteen selections the A's made in 2002 accumulated 25.2 WAR before reaching free agency—this is an estimate of the value that they provided to the club. Our first model, which assigns a WAR of 0 to every player who never reached the major leagues, suggests that the A's should have expected these draft slots to earn about 18.8 WAR. This implies that the A's did better than expectations given their draft slots.[21] In contrast, our second model simply ignores all players who never reached the major leagues, which raises expectations. In this scenario, we compare the A's drafted players who made the majors to the expected WAR of drafted players who made the majors on other teams from similar draft slots (23.2). By this method of accounting, the A's did just slightly better than expected (Table 1).[22]

But while the A's 2002 draft slightly surpassed expectations, the draft fails to bolster the case that statistics should supersede scouting in the evaluation of amateur players. Fully 89 percent of the WAR accumulated by these

Table 1. WAR of Players Drafted by Oakland A's, 2002

Pick #	Player	WAR	Expected WAR for Major Leaguers	Expected WAR for All Drafted Players
16	Nick Swisher	12.9	6.07	4.25
24	Joe Blanton	9.5	5.33	3.08
26	John McCurdy			2.84
30	Benjamin Fritz			2.42
35	Jeremy Brown	0	4.46	1.98
37	Stephen Obenchain			1.82
39	Mark Teahen	0.7	4.18	1.68
67	Steve Stanley			0.54
98	Bill Murphy	0.2	1.60	0.16
128	John Baker	1.9	0.99	0.05
158	Mark Kiger	0	0.61	0.01
188	Brian Stavisky			0
218	Brant Colamarino			0
	Total	25.2	23.2	18.8

thirteen players drafted by the A's was earned by just two players: Swisher and Blanton, both of whom were first-round picks on the basis of traditional scouting. Swisher—the son of a former major leaguer—was a no-doubt first rounder coveted by several teams. Chicago White Sox GM Kenny Williams, a former player who is notably agnostic toward sabermetrics, told Beane he was going to draft Blanton.[23]

Lewis also depicts a sharp conflict between Beane and scouting director Grady Fuson over amateur pitcher David Beck. Not surprisingly, Beane prevails and Beck is signed by the A's. As evidence of the perspicacity of Beane's statistical methods, Lewis gloats that Beck "went out and dominated the Arizona rookie league."[24] Unfortunately for the A's, the rookie league was the only thing Beck ever dominated. He never pitched above single A ball and was out of baseball by 2003.

According to Lewis, Beane didn't have "the slightest interest" in Scott Kazmir, because he was a high school player.[25] Kazmir was a dominant starting pitcher for several years for the Tampa Bay Rays, with an average WAR of 4.3 during 2005–2007. While the A's were willing to indulge in the unathletic Jeremy Brown, they were uninterested in future all-star Prince Fielder, who was "too fat even for the Oakland A's."[26] Fielder had a pedigree that was even better than Swisher's, as the son of former home run champ Cecil Fielder.

The A's took the sabermetric observation that college picks had a higher success rate than high school picks (principally because the level of competition was higher in college and, hence, player statistics were somewhat more meaningful) and made it religious dogma. No matter how much the tools of a high school player impressed the scouts, Beane wanted nothing to do with them. Lewis reports that after high school pitcher Jeremy Bonderman was selected by the A's as the twenty-sixth pick of the 2001 draft, Billy Beane threw a fit: "Billy erupted from his chair, grabbed [the phone] and hurled it right through the wall."[27] Beane traded Bonderman to Detroit during the 2002 season (in the Carlos Peña deal). Bonderman went on to have a solid eight-year career with the Tigers, averaging a WAR of 3.9 during 2004–2005, and starting Game 4 of the 2006 World Series.[28]

Unfortunately for Lewis, his prescience about the 2002 draft is almost universally off-base. He writes: "The selections made [in the 2002 draft] are, from the A's point of view, delightfully mad. Eight of the first nine teams select high schoolers. The worst teams in baseball, the teams that can least afford for their draft to go wrong, have walked into the casino, ignored the odds, and made straight for the craps table."[29]

In reality, only six, not eight, of the first nine picks were high schoolers, and of those six, three went on to become future stars (B. J. Upton, Prince Fielder, and Zack Greinke).[30] The first overall pick, Bryan Bullington by the Pirates, turned out to be one of the worst in history, despite Lewis's remark that "at least [he's] a college player."[31] In retrospect, the first nine selections of the 2002 draft serve as a reminder of why teams draft high school players: because that's where the top talent is most often available.[32]

It warrants mentioning that Bill James has long held that the level of play is too low and too uneven to be able to make much out of performance statistics in intercollegiate baseball. To be sure, college stats generally mean more than high school stats, but that is different than saying one can lean on them entirely to make draft decisions. James did develop major league equivalency conversions between different levels of minor league ball and the majors, but we believe these to be incomplete and imperfect gauges of major league potential. At best, they project what happens to the average minor league and average major league player. A useful analogy here is between a Ferrari and a Corolla both driving on an interstate at 70 miles per hour. Would this mean that in an open road race we would predict the two cars would finish in a dead heat?

In any event, Beane seems to have changed his tune on the desirability of high school picks: between 2002 and 2011 the A's had twenty-two first-round picks and all of them were college players; in 2012, their three first-round picks were all high school players.

The Lineage of Sabermetrics

Lewis's storytelling works better with simplicity and with heroes. Billy Beane was a likely suspect—a former highly touted ballplayer, good looking, and smart enough to get a baseball scholarship offer from Stanford. Another hero was Bill James, folksy, rambunctious, a gifted scribe, and self-made man who came along at the right moment (the advent of free agency and exploding player salaries, along with the maturation of the computer and the Internet). James played an important role in popularizing the use of statistics to provide new insights into understanding the value of player performance and game strategy.

The real history of baseball statistics, however, is a good deal richer and more involved than Lewis would have us believe. While Lewis makes a fleeting reference to antecedents to the work of Bill James, he does not acknowledge either the significant intellectual development of such thought or the fact that it was put into practice in the major leagues at various times. The reality is that Bill James never claimed to invent baseball analytics, and he didn't. Many of James's insights were developed years earlier by others. Nonetheless, James did suggest the term "sabermetrics," advance the sophistication of statistical analysis, and help significantly to spread its practice.

The initial introduction of statistics for analyzing the game can be traced to Henry Chadwick, who pioneered the box score (such as it was) back in the 1860s. In 1872, Chadwick proposed a measure, similar to Bill James's "range factor," as the proper way to assess fielding prowess.[33] In Chadwick's day, walks were uncommon (depending on the year, between five and nine balls were necessary for a walk), so it would not have made sense to emphasize on-base percentage. But Chadwick did emphasize the importance of not making an out, as opposed to the importance of getting a hit—a prominent feature of modern sabermetric analysis.

At the beginning of the twentieth century, baseball writer F. C. Lane denounced batting average as a meaningless metric, calling it "worse than worthless" and signaling the importance both of walks and extra base hits. In 1916, he penned the question: "Would a system that placed nickels, dimes, quarters and 50-cent pieces on the same basis be much of a system whereby to compute a man's financial resources?"[34] Lane tracked the play-by-play of sixty-two games and found the following run value to hits: singles = .457 runs; doubles = .786 runs; triples = 1.15 runs; and home runs = 1.55 runs. A single not only meant that a batter reached first base, but it also meant that any existing runners advanced a base or more, and it provided the possibility for at least one additional batter to be up that inning. Similar reasoning applies to extra base hits and, thus, a home run on average increased the number of runs scored per inning by roughly 50 percent more than 1. This analysis by Lane, from 1917, was a clear precursor to James's metric of Runs Created and the concept of linear weights.

While GM of the Brooklyn Dodgers, baseball innovator Branch Rickey, hired Allan Roth in 1944 as the first team statistician in baseball.[35] Roth's work convinced Rickey to use OBP as the basis for evaluating a batter's talent, and his analysis was instrumental in convincing the Dodgers to trade Dixie Walker as well as to bat Jackie Robinson in the cleanup position. Based on Roth's theories, Rickey published a ten-page article in *Life* magazine in 1954 that argued for a new way to assess baseball performance. The article came complete with a complex mathematical formula whose first two terms basically represented OPS (Offensive Performance Statistic = OBP + SLG), another staple of the modern sabermetric toolbox.[36]

Whether inspired by Roth and Rickey or not, Casey Stengel displayed his own adumbration of moneyball when he periodically wrote slow-footed, but high on-base guys, Norm Cerv and Elston Howard, into the leadoff spot on the lineup card.

The intellectual side of baseball analytics was given another boost in the 1950s and early 1960s by the work of George Lindsey. Lindsey developed an early version of the run expectancy matrix (discussed in the Appendix). Following the statistical work of Lane, Lindsey found slightly different run values or weights for hits (singles = .41, doubles = .82, triples = 1.06, home runs = 1.42). He also estimated the positive effect of platooning and the uncertain value of sacrifice bunts and stolen bases.[37]

After Lindsey came Earnshaw Cook. In 1964, Cook published his classic *Percentage Baseball,* the first book-length treatise on applying statistical analysis and probability theory to game strategy and player performance. Cook's volume and its sequel yielded many insights (as well as some wacky strategy suggestions), but, unfortunately, used idiosyncratic and abstruse mathematical notation that made it difficult to understand even for math Ph.D.s. Among other things, Cook developed a concept he called the Scoring Index that emphasized the importance of on-base percentage and slugging. Preeminent sportswriter Frank Deford discovered Cook's work and wrote a piece about him in *Sports Illustrated*.[38] According to Alan Schwarz, Astros GM Tal Smith, Orioles, Mariners, and Red Sox GM Lou Gorman, and manager Davey Johnson all read Cook or were made aware of his theories.[39]

Cook's work was followed by Harlan and Eldon Mills, who published *Player Win Averages: A Computer Guide* in 1972. The Mills brothers, using data from the 1970 season, developed a program that estimated how much each player's hits increased their team's probability of winning the game and developed a parallel metric. Harlan and Eldon Mills were invited to meet with executives from the Yankees and the Mets, but they were never asked to do any formal consulting and there is no evidence that their metric was ever put into practice.

Earl Weaver was hired by Orioles' owner Jerry Huffberger to manage the team in 1968.[40] Weaver had noticed during his playing days, entirely in the minor leagues, that there were some mediocre pitchers he couldn't hit at all and some really good pitchers against whom he had great success. He didn't know why. He just knew it was true and that the pattern kept repeating itself. When he became manager, he went to the Orioles' public relations director, Bob Brown, and asked him to provide match-up data on note cards between the Orioles' batters and the opposing pitchers. Soon, Weaver was also using note cards with data on opposing batters versus his pitchers. Weaver became famous for using opposite-handed platoons. Over time he began to develop other theories and tested them. He grew suspicious of the sacrifice bunt and stolen base, and came to be associated with the cliché "a walk, a blooper, and a three-run homer."[41] Weaver's emphasis on not wasting outs anticipated one of the best known sabermetric mantras.

As Weaver entered the twilight of his managerial career, other teams started to take notice of the strategic role of statistics. In 1979, Tal Smith, GM of the Houston Astros, hired sabermetrician Steve Mann to do statistical analysis. Around 1980, the San Francisco Giants hired statistical analyst Eric Walker. Walker attributes his interest in baseball analytics to reading *Percentage Baseball* by Earnshaw Cook. In 1981, the Texas Rangers hired Craig Wright, whose business card read "Sabermetrician." In 1982, Sandy Alderson, then GM of the A's, hired Walker to do statistical reports for the team. Walker continued to work with Alderson into the 1990s and wrote the pamphlet that Alderson used to indoctrinate Beane into sabermetrics.[42]

The late 1970s and early 1980s, of course, were the years when Bill James was writing his yearly *Baseball Abstract*, and Pete Palmer and John Thorn were helping to spread the sabermetric gospel through their 1984 classic *The Hidden Game of Baseball*. Palmer had been doing sophisticated statistical analysis of baseball since the 1960s, but it wasn't until he hooked up with John Thorn, and Bill James had aroused general interest, that Palmer's linear weights model and other insights found publication.[43]

Soon after Dan Duquette became GM of the Montreal Expos in September 1991 he hired statistical analyst Mike Gimbel. During the early 1980s, Duquette had worked as an assistant scout for the Milwaukee Brewers and had met Dan Okrent, who was working on his book *Nine Innings*, about one game of the Brewers' 1982 season. Okrent turned Duquette on to the emerging literature in sabermetrics that eventually led to his hiring of Gimbel. When Duquette went from Montreal to the Red Sox in 1994, he took Gimbel with him.

Meanwhile, Larry Lucchino, GM of the Baltimore Orioles at the time, hired Eddie Epstein in 1986. When Lucchino went to the Padres in 1995, Epstein went with him.

All these hires of statistical analysts in the 1970s, 1980s, and 1990s, of course, predated Beane's hiring of Paul DePodesta in November 1998, yet Lewis sets DePodesta's employment with the A's as marking a watershed for sabermetrics. Lewis does recognize in passing some of the earlier hires, but he dismisses their significance, claiming that they were outside the decision-making apparatus and had "cult" status.

While it is true that DePodesta had a more significant role than his predecessors, those who came before him were not marginalized and insignificant. As we have seen, Eric Walker had a profound effect not only on Sandy Alderson but also on Billy Beane. Alan Schwarz avers that Walker had a role in creating the world champion A's teams during 1988–1991.[44] Duquette states that Mike Gimbel was involved in giving player acquisition advice, and Lucchino says that Eddie Epstein participated in meetings about personnel issues.[45] Apparently, Epstein's advice was instrumental in the Orioles acquiring Brady Anderson. Epstein urged the move because of Anderson's high walk rate.[46]

Given the long intellectual and practical history of statistical analysis guiding player moves and strategy in baseball, and the uncertain impact that sabermetrics had on the A's success in the early 2000s, the question arises: Did Billy Beane innovate in this field?

Our answer is that while Beane significantly extended the application of sabermetrics, he did not innovate in its use. Beane also extended the use of "moneyball", understood to mean the specific application of sabermetrics in order to identify market inefficiencies (bargains), but here too previous GMs also combed new statistics to find undervalued players. Indeed, Sandy Alderson himself was seeking bargains for the A's even while Wally Haas was still the owner prior to 1995.

Other Issues

Three other matters from *Moneyball* cry out for discussion: the inconsistent characterization of Beane's methods; the accuracy of the implied predictions in the Lewis approach; and, the role of moneyball in addressing the competitive balance problem in major league baseball.

Is Moneyball Science or Instinct?

The subtitle of *Moneyball* is "The Art of Winning an Unfair Game"; the title of chapter six is "The Science of Winning an Unfair Game."[47] Is it an art or a science? Lewis can't have it both ways.

Lewis is clear from the beginning that "reason, even science, was what Billy Beane was intent on bringing to baseball."[48] The confusion continues when Lewis enumerates Beane's five simple rules for success. Rule 3 is: "Know exactly what every player in baseball is worth to you. You can put a dollar figure on it."[49] This rule, along with the other four, suggests that there is something systematic, if not scientific, behind Beane's practice of moneyball.[50] As we will discuss in later chapters, the notion that one can know "exactly" what a player (let alone every player) is worth is fanciful in the extreme. Yet, since, according to Lewis, Beane actually tries to do this, his method must be deemed to be systematic. (Others might call it delusional.) However, on the same page, Lewis opines, "His [Beane's] approach to the market for baseball players was by its nature unsystematic. Unsystematic—and yet incredibly effective." Eight pages later, Lewis writes of the Giambi-for-Mabry trade: "Billy hardly knew who Mabry was." And writing about Beane's decision not to go to the Red Sox, Lewis declares: "Billy confined himself to the usual blather about personal reasons. None of what he said was terribly rational or 'objective'—but then neither was he."[51]

Moneyball, in the final analysis, purports to be about how a team adopted a systematic, quantitative approach to player valuation that both reduced the team payroll and produced a winning team. It appears, however, that Lewis never convinced himself that Billy Beane was capable of working with such discipline and methodical commitment.[52]

In Hindsight, How Have Lewis's Contentions Held Up?

Lewis makes two sets of predictions. First, he implicitly makes various predictions about the A's selections in the 2002 draft, and also for David Beck and Jeremy Bonderman from 2001. As discussed, these have not stood the test of time.

Second, he blithely suggests easy success for J. P. Ricciardi in Toronto. Ricciardi, who also did not make it into the movie, was Alderson's special assistant from 1996 until November 2001 when he was hired by the Blue Jays to be their GM. Lewis writes that J. P. Ricciardi is "now having a ball tearing down and rebuilding his new team along the same radical lines as the Oakland A's."[53] He also quotes the Blue Jays then-CEO, Paul Godfrey, explaining why he hired Ricciardi: "Of all the people I'd talked to, J.P. was the only one with a business plan and the only one who told me, 'You are spending too much money.... If you can stand the heat in the media, I can make you cheaper and better. It'll take a couple of months to make you cheaper and a couple of years to make you better. But you'll be a lot better.'"[54] One of Ricciardi's first moves was to hire Keith Law, a twenty-eight-year-old Harvard-schooled sabermetrician and writer for Baseball Prospectus. Soon thereafter Ricciardi reportedly fired twenty-five Blue Jays scouts.[55] As we shall see, Toronto did shift toward a more sabermetric strategy under Ricciardi. The question is whether or not the new approach paid off.

During the two years prior to Ricciardi's arrival, the Blue Jays averaged

81.5 wins and a $64.4 million payroll. During the eight years under Ricciardi, 2002–2009, the Jays averaged 80.25 wins and a $72.5 million payroll.[56] The team did have a strong turnaround year in 2003, but that was due to an MVP year for first baseman Carlos Delgado, with an OPS of 1.019, 42 home runs, and 145 RBIs, as well as the emergence of star pitcher Roy Halladay and outfielder Vernon Wells. All three had been signed by the Blue Jays years before the arrival of Ricciardi. If there was some simple magical formula behind moneyball, as Lewis insinuated, then it eluded the Toronto Blue Jays.

Moneyball and Fixing Competitive Imbalance in Baseball

Lewis begins *Moneyball* by saying he fell in love with a story and goes on to copiously cite statistics about financial and on-field inequality in baseball. He implicitly mocks MLB Commissioner Bud Selig's comment that the A's success was an aberration. Rather, for Lewis, it is a David and Goliath story, and Billy Beane together with moneyball slay the giant. Moreover, Lewis hints that with moneyball principles and mentally sharp GMs, baseball's problem of competitive imbalance can be remedied. Listen to Lewis's bold characterization of what Beane believed: "The market for baseball players was so inefficient, and the general grasp of sound baseball strategy so weak, that superior management could still run circles around taller piles of cash."[57]

Even if the inefficiencies in the player market were so pronounced and the grasp of game strategy sufficiently undeveloped, and even if Billy Beane took advantage of this situation so that the small market A's were successful, it would still be a dubious proposition that sabermetric smarts could promote better competitive balance. The reason is that Lewis would have made the baseball world aware of the magic formula and the big market teams could now exploit it as well as the small market teams.[58] But, as we have seen, the available evidence does not support this premise.

Further, Lewis misapprehends the nature of imbalance in baseball. Not only does he misrepresent some relevant facts, but he seems to presume that, absent sabermetrics, high payrolls necessarily lead to winning teams.[59] In fact, the correlation between team payroll and win percentage in baseball over the past twenty years is far from determinative. As we shall elaborate in Chapter

6, the variance in win percentage explained by the variance in payroll generally has ranged between 10 and 35 percent, depending on the year. This, of course, means that between 65 and 90 percent of the variance in win percentage is explained by factors other than payroll (such as player performance, player injuries, team chemistry, intelligent management, or luck). That said, although high payroll does not guarantee success, it certainly helps.

The most common measurement of competitive balance in baseball is the standard deviation of win percentages across teams. By this metric, there is little empirical support for the claim that the spread of sabermetric knowledge after 2000 promoted greater balance. Using the ratio of standard deviation to idealized standard deviation,[60] we find that the level of competitive balance in baseball was the same during 1980–1989 and 1990–1999 with a ratio of 1.7. In what Lewis would have us believe to be the first sabermetric decade, 2000–2009, the ratio actually jumped to 1.86, suggesting less balance.

If we look a little further into the dynamic of the period, we can discern an alternative explanation of the pattern. Consider the period 1996 through 2009, broken down by the underlying three collective bargaining agreements (CBAs), 1996–2002, 2003–2006, and 2007–2009. The competitive balance ratio went from 1.89 during 1996–2002, to 1.90 during 2003–06, to 1.68 during 2007–2009. Over the course of these three CBAs, revenue sharing from baseball's rich to poor teams increased from an annual average of $107.1 million, to $278.7 million, to $396.3 million. That is, despite the almost tripling of revenue sharing between the first two CBAs, the measurement of imbalance actually increased (albeit marginally). Only with the third CBA, after a further, more modest increase in revenue sharing, did the measure of imbalance decrease.

What changed between the second and third CBAs? The incentive structure of revenue sharing shifted dramatically. During the first two CBAs, the marginal tax rates on local team revenue were actually higher on low revenue teams and lower on high revenue teams. This meant that, in addition to normal market factors, the low revenue teams had even less incentive to increase revenue than the high revenue teams. Between 2002 and 2006, every time a low revenue team increased revenue by a dollar, they lost approximately 48 cents in revenue sharing. In contrast, for every extra dollar of revenue that a high revenue team generated, it paid 39 cents into the revenue sharing pot. Thus, the underlying incentives were perverse and moved the system in the wrong direction. Only with the new CBA in 2007 was this inverted incentive system corrected, and only after 2007 was there payroll compression across the teams. The coefficient of variation of team payrolls, after rising from .397 to .435 between the 1996–2002 CBA and the 2003–2006 CBA, fell to .405 during 2007–2009.[61] The turnaround in payroll disparity, in turn, helped to promote the improvement in competitive balance.

While it is true that small market teams that effectively practice saber-metrics have a chance to make up some of the lost ground from their revenue inferiority, large market teams also have the ability to practice sabermetrics. It is also true, as we shall see, that sabermetrics, sagaciously applied, can yield a healthy bang for the buck, and that small market teams have relatively more equal access to this resource than they do to the free agent market. Sabermet-rics, then, might provide some impetus toward greater competitive balance, but the early and easy insights of baseball analytics have been exhausted. The challenges that lie ahead are formidable, so it would be prudent to expect no easy fixes. We will return to discuss related aspects of the competitive balance dynamic in Chapter 6.

Conclusion

While the book and the movie *Moneyball* can each be recognized as enter-taining, they leave a distorted picture of the baseball industry and the impact of sabermetrics.

In our view, the explosion of sabermetrics in baseball (both outside and within team front offices) was a product of several forces. There was an intel-lectual trove of sabermetric analysis in the 1970s, waiting to be exploited. Bill James's annual *Baseball Abstracts* helped to call attention to this work, as did some of the earlier on-field practitioners. The advent of free agency, in the context of industry-wide revenue growth, in baseball increased the average major league baseball salary from $51,501 in 1976, to $1.1 million in 1992, to approximately $3.3 million today. This explosion in player compensation nat-urally led front offices to seek more information on the best ways to evaluate and to exploit player talent. Importantly, the mass development of the computer, the desktop and laptop, the iPad, the smartphone and the Internet have facilitated both the gathering and processing of statistics and the emergence of myriad statistical services, and have improved accessibility to baseball data and its analysis. Finally, for all of its deficiencies, *Moneyball* did tell a good story with some underlying validity, and it reinforced the objective forces and the momentum that were already in play.

Some have grumbled that all this data is turning baseball away from a game of instincts and emotions and into a game of boring mathematical precision. Veteran sportswriter Stanley Frank published an article in *Sports Illustrated* where he groused: "The greatest menace to big-time sports today is neither the shrinking gate nor TV. . . . It is a nonsense of numbers [and] the stupefying emphasis on meaningless statistics which is draining the color from competition." Frank was writing in 1958. And Jim Murray, one of Bill James's favorite columnists, wrote in 1961: "The game of statistics has begun to run away with the game of baseball. I mean, it's not a sport anymore, it's a multiplication table with baselines."[62]

Yet, despite the statistical onslaught, baseball has only grown in popularity over the years. Statistical analysis is here to stay. The question for baseball front offices is how to most effectively combine statistical with traditional analysis. We hope to throw some light on this question in the chapters that follow.

2

The Growth and Application of Baseball Analytics Today

We have called into question many of the assertions made in *Moneyball*, and examined their veracity with the benefit of hindsight. Nevertheless, the impact that *Moneyball* has had on the baseball industry is seismic, and undeniable. The book has been massively influential within front offices from coast to coast, and has been an important catalyst for the explosion of data and analytics currently roiling the larger sports world. In this chapter, we will examine the current state of analytics in baseball, and illustrate the role that *Moneyball* has played in bringing us to this point.

The Proliferation of Analytics in Baseball

Lewis makes it clear that in 2002, the A's were, if not the only team in baseball using statistical analysis to motivate their decision-making, certainly the most aggressive. Lewis asserts that "you could count on one hand the number of 'sabermetricians' inside of baseball."[1] As we argued previously, this is a loose interpretation of reality, since pioneers like Craig Wright and Eric Walker would have certainly qualified under that distinction in years past. Nevertheless, if Lewis is correct that there were at most five sabermetricians working inside baseball in 2002, how many are there now?

Unfortunately, a precise answer to this question is probably impossible, but in what follows, we derive an estimate. The first hurdle is to define who, in fact, qualifies as a sabermetrician. What type of training is required? What job functions could she perform?

At this point, no accredited school or university offers a degree in sabermetrics or sports analytics. Moreover, one of the defining characteristics of the sabermetric movement has been the accessibility of the research conducted by those who are *not* writing for an academic audience. Most notably, Bill James's work surged in popularity due to the quality, passion, and insightfulness of his writing, not his emphasis on careful estimation and revelation of his standard errors. (James succeeded because of, rather than in spite of, his lack of formal training in statistics, and Lewis concedes that he "sometimes did violence to the laws of statistics.")[2]

Conversely, some of the most statistically sophisticated work being done in sabermetrics today, such as Shane Jensen's work on estimating fielding ability,[3] has failed to gain widespread acceptance within the community, but particularly within front offices, because you need something close to a Ph.D. in statistics to really understand it.

But we can adopt a good rule of thumb using Lewis's implied characterization of Paul DePodesta as a sabermetrician. At the time, DePodesta was the assistant general manager of the A's, the number two post in most baseball operations front offices.[4] Under this definition, DePodesta certainly would have been the highest-ranking sabermetrician in baseball history. DePodesta was an economics major at Harvard who "always had some sort of facility with numbers."[5] He certainly has the quantitative background to perform and interpret linear regression models, but, like James, lacks formal training in mathematical statistics or advanced techniques at the level of, say, hierarchical Bayesian models. This background (undergraduate social science major at an elite university with some quantitative training) is now very common among front office executives at all levels of the baseball operations hierarchy.

Using DePodesta as a guide, we have estimated the number of full-time employees working in baseball front offices whose jobs appear to be primarily analytical in nature. The results (Table 2) were obtained by scouring team media guides and talking to those who work in the game. Of course, it is very difficult to know precisely who is doing what, but any employee in a baseball department whose job title contains the word "analytic" or "statistic" is included. For the purpose of consistency, top-level executives who may be former analysts themselves, like Paul DePodesta, are not included. We have chosen to make this distinction since top-level executives are not primarily working on analytics. Rather, executives like DePodesta or Theo Epstein have no doubt incorporated sabermetrics into their philosophy, but delegate the actual number-crunching to lower-level staffers. (Later, we will examine how the assimilation of sabermetrics has paved the way for young executives like Epstein.) Again, it is important to caution that the breakdown in Table 2 is meant only to be illustrative. There may be employees without sabermetric-type titles who do analytic work and employees with sabermetric-type titles who spend only a portion of their time on such endeavors. Further, if one were to ask a baseball operations employee at any team whether they practice sabermetrics, it is likely that the answer would be affirmative. To say otherwise would be tantamount to proclaiming you are against a healthy diet. The issue we are interested in, however, is not whether someone in baseball operations looks at statistics (of course, every team does this and always has), but the nature of the statistics that are considered, how they are analyzed, and what they signify in the organization. Based on our knowledge of front offices, we believe that an initial reasonable proxy for the sabermetric orientation of a team is whether or not positions are labeled analytic or sabermetric.[6] Also, keep in mind that teams regularly add and subtract employees in all areas, so what we have presented is merely a snapshot in time.

While in 2002, there were only a handful of people working in analytics, our research indicates that today at least seventeen teams employ more than one person who focuses on analytics in some capacity, while another five teams employ one person full-time and four more have someone working part-time in this area. It can be no coincidence that most of these people have been hired since the publication of *Moneyball*, and, in some cases, the connection is directly causal.[7] Further, some if not all of the teams in the "no analytical presence" column likely have a baseball operations person who spends time either doing her own analytical work or reading and sharing the work of other statistical analysts.

Table 2. Breakdown of MLB Front Offices by Number of Full-Time Employees
Working Primarily in Analytics, 2012

Teams with at least two people working mostly on analytics (17)	Teams with one person who likely spends most of her time working on analytics (5)	Teams with one person who spends part of her time working on analytics (4)	Teams with no apparent analytical presence (4)
Tampa Bay (8)	Chicago White Sox	Arizona	Atlanta
Cleveland (5)	San Francisco	Detroit	Colorado
New York Yankees (5)	Texas	Los Angeles Angels	Miami
Boston (4)	Toronto	Minnesota	Philadelphia
Houston (4)	Washington		
Kansas City (4)			
Milwaukee (3)			
New York Mets (3)			
Pittsburgh (3)			
San Diego (3)			
St. Louis (3)			
Baltimore (2)			
Chicago Cubs (2)			
Cincinnati (2)			
Los Angeles Dodgers (2)			
Oakland (2)			
Seattle (2)			

Of course, counting the number of employees designated for analytics does not directly reflect upon *Moneyball,* since a primary innovation of the 2002 A's was not so much the number of employees devoted to sabermetrics, but rather the influence that sabermetrics had on their general manager. Today, sabermetrics is certainly highly influential in many front offices (Tampa, Boston, Cleveland, Baltimore, the New York Mets and the Yankees, and of course, Oakland, to name a few), but is almost certainly less influential among others (e.g., Miami and Philadelphia).[8] But even among those teams that employ multiple people doing analytics (e.g., Milwaukee and Cincinnati), the influence of sabermetrics on the GM's thinking may be slight.[9] We have also included some employees whose primary analytical medium may be video, as opposed to statistics.[10]

We feel the inclusion of video analytics is warranted, because a growing trend in front offices is to replace the traditional advance scout, who follows the team's schedule one or two series in advance and writes detailed reports on the tendencies of their upcoming opponents, with one or more front office employees who accomplish this same task by blending analysis of both statistics and video. While this change in policy is often written off as a cost-costing measure, the true innovator in this respect was likely DePodesta himself, who started his career as an advance scout for the Indians. He recalls that his motivation for sabermetric self-education grew out of a desire to overcome what he perceived to be his own shortcomings in traditional scouting. In any event, it is largely due to the ambiguity of the relationship between counting employees and the true development and emphasis on sabermetric practice that we seek a more objective and quantitative measure of team sabermetric intensity in Chapter 7.

Although almost all of those working in analytics hold an undergraduate degree, a master's degree in statistics is not uncommon, especially among those who have risen to mid-level positions such as "senior quantitative analyst"[11] or "manager, baseball analytics."[12] Farhan Zaidi, who earned a doctorate in behavioral economics at UC-Berkeley before becoming the director of baseball operations for the Oakland A's (usually the number three post), is the highest-ranking of just a couple of front office employees with a Ph.D.[13]

Among the teams more aggressive with their employment, an expanded version of the R&D model described in *Moneyball* seems to have gained some currency.[14] Under the direction of former Goldman Sachs partner Stuart Sternberg, the Tampa Bay Rays now employ at least eight people contributing to their analytics department.[15] The top-down model consists of three systems developers, two baseball operations assistants, and two junior analysts working under the director of baseball research and development James Click (a Yale graduate who got his start writing for Baseball Prospectus, an online source for sabermetric articles and statistics). The Yankees, Indians, and Red Sox have a similar, but leaner, structure in place.

The attraction of working for a major league front office is obvious, but the depth of the pool of candidates may surprise some. Many candidates come from Lewis's previous industry, finance, which certainly offers a broad overlap in skill set but retains most of its talent by offering vastly more lucrative monetary rewards than baseball. Lewis describes DePodesta as fitting the finance industry mold, "but the market for baseball players, in Paul's [DePodesta's] view, was far more interesting than anything Wall Street offered."[16] Sig Mejdal, now director of decision sciences for the Houston Astros, was a NASA engineer before descending on the winter meetings in search of a job. In the opposite direction, Nate Silver honed his skills in predictive analytics by building a projection system for Baseball Prospectus before becoming one of the world's best-known political forecasters for FiveThirtyEight.com, and now the *New York Times*.

Infiltration and Assimilation of "Stat Guys"

To develop what is one of the more compelling and accessible themes in *Moneyball*, Lewis goes to great lengths to characterize the philosophy of Billy Beane, DePodesta, and especially Bill James, as being antithetical to the conventional wisdom that controlled baseball. In Lewis's view, although Beane and DePodesta were working within the sport, what they were doing was unusual, and in some respects unprecedented. James was a more typical outsider—a vocal minority preaching a gospel that fell mostly on deaf front office ears hiding behind "very effective walls [that] keep out everything."[17] Lewis casts the conflict within the baseball industry as being between the "superior management" effected by Beane (motivated by the insights of James) and the Luddite conventional wisdom embodied by his scouts.[18] According to Lewis, Bill James believed that he is "right and the world is wrong," and bemoaned the prevailing "anti-intellectual resentment."[19] Thus, the adherents of sabermetrics, both inside and outside the baseball industry, were easily identified misfits relegated to the fringes of the established power structure.

In this respect, a great deal has changed since the publication of *Moneyball*, as believers in sabermetrics have been rapidly assimilated into the baseball industry. An understanding of baseball analytics was not merely a plus, but a requirement for the GM jobs that went to Theo Epstein in Boston and Andrew Friedman in Tampa Bay. In 2003 the St. Louis Cardinals hired Jeff Luhnow, a true baseball outsider with an MBA from Northwestern, and tasked him with overseeing a team of statistical consultants. By the time Luhnow left the Cardinals to become the GM of the Houston Astros, he was supervising the Cardinals entire scouting and player development system and was touted for his "scouting acumen."[20] DePodesta now serves in a similar role with the Mets, overseeing amateur scouting and player development, but spends much of his time on the road, personally scouting amateur players. Keith Law was one of the few analysts working in baseball before *Moneyball*, having been hired by Toronto GM (and former A's director of player development) J. P. Ricciardi. But since leaving the Blue Jays in 2007, Law has made a living writing for ESPN.com, drawing most of his material from scouting amateur and minor league prospects.

The surest sign of the assimilation of sabermetrics into the baseball industry is that it is no longer clear whose bread is buttered by statistics, and whose by traditional scouting. Carlos Gomez, currently the director of international scouting for the Arizona Diamondbacks, was a former minor league pitcher. But his path to the front office was paved writing articles for Baseball Prospectus on pitching mechanics.[21] Adam Fisher of the Mets, another Harvard graduate, has filled a variety of roles within the baseball operations department, including working in an analytical capacity in the front office, as a professional scout in the field, and as an advance scout combining video and statistical analysis. Galen Carr left Salomon Smith Barney in 2000 to join the Red Sox front office, but now serves as a professional scout based out of his home in Burlington, Vermont. [22] These are just three more examples of people working within the game who have happily married the analytical mindset outlined in *Moneyball* as "heretical" with an understanding of traditional scouting set up in the book as adversarial.[23] As we discussed in Chapter 1, the strict dichotomy between the two approaches depicted in *Moneyball* was always an inaccurate hyperbole.[24]

The Blogosphere

By 1988, Bill James had stopped publishing his annual *Abstract*, and yet by the time *Moneyball* was published in 2003, sabermetrics had already taken root among a few front offices and many more fans. Specifically, ground-breaking theories like Vörös McCracken's Defense Independent Pitching Statistics were communicated to Paul DePodesta via Baseball Prospectus.[25] The void left by James was filled in print form by two SABR publications: the *Baseball Research Journal*; and *By the Numbers*, the newsletter of the SABR Statistical Analysis committee. But by the late 1990s, what is true today had already become obvious: the Internet had an unparalleled ability to disseminate ideas and information widely and quickly. Perhaps most important for a burgeoning, data-heavy field like sabermetrics, one could receive nearly instant feedback on statistical analysis from virtually anyone in the world who was interested. In this incubator, sabermetrics grew rapidly.

Critical to this explosion were two open sources of baseball data: the LahmanDB, a database curated by journalist Sean Lahman that contained statistics for every major league player in each season since 1871; and Retrosheet, a collection of archived play-by-play accounts maintained by biology professor Dave Smith. The former is small (on the order of several megabytes), but is well-packaged, easy to understand, and contains as much information as *Total Baseball* or any other desktop reference. While a math professor at Saint Joseph's University, Sean Forman created a web front-end to the LahmanDB that became the hugely popular Baseball-Reference.com site. The website allowed anyone to quickly answer questions that would otherwise have required an extensive baseball card collection (e.g., in how many seasons did Mickey Mantle hit forty or more home runs?). The database, however, allowed sabermetricians to compute any statistic they could think of for any (and all) players in major league history and quickly sort the results. To illustrate the order of magnitude difference in computational ability at play here, imagine answering the question, "How many players with at least 1,000 hits have more home runs than doubles in their career?" There are 1,217 players with 1,000 or more career hits, so to count the ones who qualify using a website would take at least 1,217 clicks. But this question can be answered in seconds through a well-written query to the LahmanDB.[26]

The Retrosheet data is voluminous (on the order of several gigabytes), but it contains detailed play-by-play data going back to the 1940s. Working with Retrosheet data is more cumbersome, since it requires manipulating customized text-processing tools, but the scope of questions that can be addressed is virtually limitless. For example, the LahmanDB provides no information about individual games, batter-versus-pitcher matchups, or situational statistics. But a well-oiled Retrosheet database can make quick work of incredibly specific questions (e.g., did Mickey Mantle hit better in the fifth inning of home games with a runner on third and less than two outs on even or odd numbered days?).[27] Thanks to these data sources and online venues like Baseball Prospectus, work that would have taken James hours of painstaking calculation and self-publishing could be performed by a college student in a matter of minutes on a laptop in his dorm room, and sent around the world overnight. Accordingly, the pace of sabermetric activity and the potential for its assimilation swiftly increased.

When James joined the front office of the Red Sox in 2003, it presaged a flood of talent from the sabermetric community to the baseball industry. Sabermetrically inclined executives like Theo Epstein and Paul DePodesta were now running major league clubs, and they needed assistants who could perform cutting-edge analysis for them. As the most prominent venue for the exchange of sabermetric ideas, Baseball Prospectus became a clearinghouse for young sabermetric talent. BP alum Keith Law was already working for the Toronto Blue Jays when *Moneyball* was published, but in the years that followed James Click joined the Rays, Keith Woolner joined the Indians, Dan Fox joined the Pirates, and more recently, Mike Fast and former BP managing partner Kevin Goldstein left for the Astros. Mercifully, there was no shortage of talent being funneled to BP itself. Students who had been exposed to sabermetrics in college could parlay a well-written article or two for BP into a highly sought-after internship with a major league club. The jobs did not pay well, but they sometimes led to full-time jobs (most of which also didn't pay well). The demand for sabermetric content online was so great that numerous sites sprung up around BP: FanGraphs, Hardball Times, Baseball Analysts, and many other websites provided articles with new thoughts, new metrics, and new venues for discussion every day. By the late 2000s, early BP members like Law and Will Carroll were respected journalists carrying cards of the Baseball Writers Association of America, and the voting privileges that go with them. In less than ten years, sabermetric bloggers had moved from the fringes of the Internet to the press box, and scratched out the line separating them from newspaper columnists.

But while the blogosphere has played a catalytic role in expanding the reach of sabermetrics, its stewardship of sabermetric theory has been more complicated. The decentralized nature of online communication has produced thousands of articles, with a relatively democratic vetting process. With the open data sources mentioned above and the computational power of just about any decent computer, barriers to enter the field are low. Moreover, few sabermetric articles require any understanding of statistics beyond what you would likely be exposed to in an introductory statistics class—mainly because most sabermetric practitioners have not had any statistical training beyond this level. This has led to very creative approaches to difficult questions. However, one downside to this decentralization has been an outpouring of acronyms that do little other than confuse even habitual sabermetric readers. For example, we have chosen to use BABIP as shorthand for "batting average on balls in play," but nearly as many others (including Vörös McCracken) continue to refer to this exact same concept as "hits per balls in play" and use the abbreviation HPBP. Further, while it is undoubtedly true that the avoidance of statistical terminology has made sabermetric research accessible to many who would not otherwise follow, it has hindered the development of a coherent body of sabermetric theory. As a result, modeling decisions that are justified by theory are presented as if they were made ad hoc.

More important, the foundation of scientific research is reproducibility. And because much of the sabermetric work published online is derived from open data sources, it is particularly well suited to exact reproduction. While it is true that scientific terminology presents a barrier to many, its purpose is to streamline the intake of new ideas by those who wish to verify the details. Sabermetrics literature sometimes seems caught between two audiences: a lay audience that wants to know the results of a study without the details; and a technical audience that wants to verify the details. Research in many fields is presented in both venues simultaneously, where a technical paper is sent to a peer-reviewed journal, but a more accessible paper is released to the public. The *Journal of Quantitative Analysis in Sports* has helped in this respect, but in our view the gap between the online sabermetric community and the academic sabermetric community is too large. There are too many good ideas floating around in each venue that are not being translated to the other.

Technology and Big Data

The relationship between statistics and baseball is long and storied, but the adoption of technology within baseball continues to be fraught with roadblocks. Discussion about expanding the use of instant replay during games continues to be a major topic at the owners' meetings each fall, and while some progress has been made, the subject continues to be divisive. Behind the scenes, many front offices are still struggling to effectively integrate technology into their baseball operations staff. Still, all scouts are now equipped with smartphones in addition to radar guns, and some use tablets instead of laptops for entering their reports. But a more interesting evolution is taking place within team offices, where a new kind of employee is setting up shop. In scouting and player development, the same kinds of people as before are getting the new jobs (former players mostly)—but they may be expected to use new tools. Conversely, in many front offices entry-level positions are being filled by young staffers who would likely have had no claim to a front office job as recently as the 1990s—they would have been more likely to be found in an information technology department, or on Wall Street.

With an eye undoubtedly honed through his own background in finance, Lewis sees DePodesta as an early embodiment of this trend: "Everywhere one turned in competitive markets, technology was offering the people who understood it an edge. What was happening to capitalism should have happened to baseball: the technical man with his analytical magic should have risen to prominence in baseball management, just as he was rising to prominence on, say, Wall Street."[28]

Consider how Lewis's words have been put into action since *Moneyball*. John Henry bought the Red Sox in 2002 with money he made building quantitative financial models, and after whiffing on Billy Beane himself, gave the reins to a twenty-eight-year-old Theo Epstein, and hired James to be a key advisor. When Stuart Sternberg assumed control of the Rays in 2005, he installed Andrew Friedman—a former Bear Stearns analyst with no previous experience in baseball—as his GM.[29] To say that those two hires were successful is an understatement. Between them they produced two World Series rings, another appearance, and a Sporting New Executive of the Year Award. Indeed, Lewis's "technical man" rose to prominence in baseball more or less immediately after he wrote the words in the passage above.

In the years that have followed, more and more talent that might otherwise have been headed to Mountain View or Wall Street has flowed to Yawkey Way. Ironically, sabermetrically inclined executives like Beane and Indians GM Chris Antonetti already see themselves as future casualties of this migration, In Beane's words: "The people who are coming into the game, the creativity, the intelligence—it's unparalleled right now. In ten years if I applied for this job I wouldn't even get an interview."[30] Antonetti, who lacks professional playing experience, is also astounded by the quality of the resumes he sees today, and attributes the influx of talent directly to *Moneyball*.[31] There will always be a place in the front office for intelligent former players, but there are a few more places now for everyone else.

Moreover, the skills necessary to perform sabermetric analysis have changed. Whereas many of those associated with sabermetrics at the higher levels had degrees in the social sciences and used a spreadsheet as their weapon of choice, today's entry-level sabermetricians are more likely to have a degree in applied mathematics or computer science and come writing their own code. Again, to illustrate the difference in the order of magnitude of the problems each can solve, until recently Microsoft Excel was limited to 65,536 (i.e., 2^{16}) rows of data, and even the current version is limited to a little more than 1 million rows. In contrast, commonly used database management systems like MySQL can easily store many millions of rows. This distinction has become relevant to baseball in just the past few years, as the deluge of play-by-play and even pitch-by-pitch data has overwhelmed clubs.[32] Thankfully, baseball's data onslaught is merely a trickle compared to the flood faced by large Internet companies like Google, Facebook, and Amazon. The technological ecosystem that supports these companies is a powerful library from which baseball teams can borrow, often for free.

The buzzword for the enormous data processed by companies like Google is "big data," while the field devoted to studying modern data analysis techniques is known as "data science." The former is distinguished by data streams that are three orders of magnitude larger than what major league clubs are currently storing (two if you include video). However, the introduction of FIELDf/x data has the potential to shrink that gap to two (one with video). Nevertheless, many baseball operations departments are investing in computer hardware to build data centers that rival those of the entire organization's IT department. Others, recognizing their limited ability to keep up with the pace of technology, are paying six figures per season to outsource the job of warehousing, analyzing, and displaying their data to Bloomberg Sports, an offshoot of the financial giant.[33]

Conversely, sabermetrics is very much a popular embodiment of data science. Data science is distinguished from statistics through its heavier emphasis on data, its reliance upon programming techniques common in computer science but rare in classical statistics, and the importance of incorporating extensive "domain knowledge" (specific knowledge of the subject being studied) into the analysis. Sabermetricians practice this exactly: they frequently work with large, sometimes messy databases that require customized code to manage, and their knowledge of baseball is integral to formulating a model that is applicable to the problem of interest. This happy coincidence is exactly what enables a successful practitioner of sabermetrics like Nate Silver to seamlessly migrate his data science skills to other application areas. Moreover, it provides an accessible venue for higher-education courses that equip graduates with skills applicable to a variety of fields. Accordingly, classes in sabermetrics have spring up at Williams College (alma mater of former Mets and Orioles GM Jim Duquette), Tufts University, and Bowling Green State University, among others.

The Third Parties: Symbiotic or Parasitic?

At its core, *Moneyball* was about a market inefficiency, and as we will show in Chapter 7, the market inefficiency the A's exploited in the early 2000s is now likely closed. We showed above that more front-office talent is now devoted to analytics than ever before, but we will present evidence in Chapter 7 that

suggests that sabermetrics is working, and thus the $60,000 statistical ana-
lyst more than makes up for his own salary in cost savings to the club. But
this analyst is limited by the quality of his resources, be they in the form of
data, hardware, storage, or software. This observation was made years ago by
a whole host of third-party vendors who provide a variety of services in a des-
perate attempt to get a piece of the major league pie. Every year at the winter
meetings, a massive trade show is held where hundreds of such companies
vie for the attention of baseball front offices. Are these companies part of a
symbiotic ecosystem surrounding analytics? Or are they capitalist parasites
depleting the limited resources of MLB clubs?

The most precious resource to a statistical analyst is data, and a variety of
companies have been licensing data to major league clubs for decades. From
the ashes of Project Scoresheet, a group initiated by Bill James, two parallel data
organizations arose: the aforementioned Retrosheet, a nonprofit that provides
its data for free; and STATS LLC (better known as STATS, Inc.), a private company founded by John Dewan, a frequent business associate of James's. While
Retrosheet continued in the grassroots tradition of Project Scoresheet, cobbling
play-by-play data together from newspaper accounts and donated scoresheets,
STATS became a multimillion-dollar global sports information provider, part-
nering with industry giants like ESPN and the NBA.[34] Meanwhile, Dave Smith
runs Retrosheet for $10 per month in web hosting fees.[35]

After Dewan sold his interest in STATS in 1999, he got back into the baseball data game with Baseball Info Solutions, which has been competing with
STATS in the proprietary data market since the early to mid-2000s. The data
provided by these private companies was superior to the data provided by
Retrosheet, primarily because it could be uploaded daily and included information about the location, velocity, and pitch type of nearly every pitch
thrown.[36] A full season feed cost a major league club tens of thousands of
dollars, and as the number of teams licensing the data increased, the clubs got
wiser. By 2006, Major League Baseball Advanced Media, a limited partnership
of the club owners, was providing analogous data, including PITCHf/x data
collected by Sportvision, to the major league clubs at no additional charge.[37]
While there were undoubtedly teams that still had little interest in this type of
data, this turn of events suggests that enough of the major league clubs were

interested so as to forego an expensive proprietary advantage (licensing the data from a third party) to achieve an economy of scale.

With MLBAM cannibalizing play-by-play and pitch-by-pitch data revenue, the third-party providers have invented new products. Sportvision licenses its PITCHf/x data to MLBAM to disseminate to the clubs, but maintains separate relationships for other sources of data, such as HITf/x, which tracks the muzzle velocity and trajectory of batted balls coming off of the bat, and COMMANDf/x, which measures the magnitude and direction of how far a pitcher missed his spot (i.e., how far the catcher had to move his glove). Trackman uses radar technology (in contrast to Sportvision's camera technology) to measure the spin rate and flight time of pitches. TruMedia provides not data, but a user interface to data, via an interactive web application useful for advance scouting. Since many clubs had already allocated money for baseball analytics, the economy of scale achieved through MLBAM simply allowed them to spend their money on other products. What is unclear at this point is how much meaningful information the clubs are getting from these third-party products. By 2013, DePodesta began to question not the importance of data analysis, but the value of the data onslaught, writing, "more data is not always better data. What we are seeking is relevant data."[38]

Conclusion

In this chapter we have demonstrated that front offices have many more people now working on baseball analytics than ever before. In particular, more than half of the thirty clubs have more than one person who is primarily working on analytics, and just four clubs appear to have little or no analytical presence. At the same time, more and better data is flowing to clubs, who are spending money either to upgrade their technological infrastructure or to outsource that job to a third-party company. But whereas at the time of *Moneyball*, the A's had just a few employees who were craving for more and better data so that they could figure out what they wanted to know, the challenge in today's front offices is to find enough employees who are capable of extracting meaningful information from what is quickly becoming a torrent of data. The greatest unknown, and perhaps the source of the next market inefficiency, is how clubs will meet that challenge.

3

An Overview of Current Sabermetric Thought I

Offense

In the next two chapters we will present an overview of the current state of baseball analytics, while making careful attempts to compare the current results to those that were mentioned in *Moneyball*. Our emphasis is on exposition, in that we will attempt to explain and justify the basics of sabermetric theory to the reader. Although much lies beyond the scope of what we can accomplish here, a thorough reading should give the interested reader a firm grasp of how sabermetricians think about the game, and demystify some important results that are mentioned in passing in both *Moneyball* and the popular media.

Why Do Teams Win Games?

For those new to sabermetrics, one of the most eye-opening passages in *Moneyball*, the book, begins with Paul DePodesta "reducing the coming six months to a math problem."[1] To accomplish this, DePodesta estimates four quantities:

1. the number of wins likely necessary to make the playoffs (about 95);
2. the number of runs by which the A's need to outscore their opponents over the course of the season in order to win that many games (about 135);

3. the number of runs that the A's, as currently constituted, are likely
   to score (810 ± 10); and,

4. the number of runs that the A's, as currently constituted, are likely
   to allow (660 ± 10).

The answers to the last two questions allow DePodesta to determine whether the A's will reach the threshold in the first question. Lewis mentions parenthetically the missing piece of the equation: a strong relationship between the number of runs that a team scores and allows over the course of the season, and the number of games that they win. This may seem obvious, but keep in mind that we are only talking about the *cumulative* number of runs scored and allowed over the course of a season, with no information about the distribution of how those runs are scored in any particular game.

The relationship to which Lewis alludes is known, somewhat misleadingly, as the Pythagorean Expectation, and it is one of Bill James's more enduring contributions to the field of sabermetrics. James created a simple but nonlinear statistical model that relates runs scored (RS) and runs allowed (RA) to a team's expected winning percentage (WPCT):

$$\text{WPCT} = \frac{\text{RS}^2}{\text{RS}^2 + \text{RA}^2} = \frac{1}{1 + (^{\text{RA}}\!/_{\text{RS}})^2}$$

James described his formula as Pythagorean because the sum of squared terms reminded him of the Pythagorean Theorem ($a^2 + b^2 = c^2$, where a and b are the lengths of the shorter sides of a right triangle, and c is the length of the hypotenuse). But this similarity was largely a coincidence. While James undoubtedly used the exponent of 2 (the solid line in Figure 1) for convenience and simplicity, later sabermetricians sought a more precise, less arbitrary value, and found that as the game has changed over the years, the value of the exponent that best fits the data has changed with it. For clarity, we show (dotted line) that the exponent that best fits the data from all team-seasons since 1954 is about 1.85.[2]

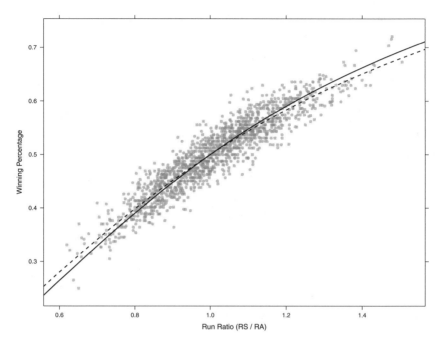

Figure 1. Winning Percentage Versus Run Ratio, 1954–2011
Each dot represents one team in one season, and all teams from 1954–2011 are represented (the dots are partially transparent, so a darker cluster indicates that more dots are present). The solid line shows James's model for expected winning percentage as a function of a team's run ratio (with an exponent of 2). The dashed line shows the best fit model (with an exponent of about 1.85).

It is worth reiterating that James's formula defines an *expected* winning percentage, based on the known ratio of runs scored to runs allowed. Since the formula seems to work so well in practice, it is commonly used to estimate a team's projected finish midway through the season, given its current run ratio. For example, it is not uncommon for a baseball team to be several games over .500 at the All-Star break, but have been outscored on the season. If we assume that this team will continue to score and allow runs at the same rates, then by James's formula, the expected winning percentage for that team in the second half would be under .500. Thus, the team's expected final winning percentage would include the number of games they had actually won, plus the expectation that they would win less than half of their remaining games.

Naturally, deviations from this expected winning percentage are the subject of some debate. The standard deviation between the expected and actual wins is about four games, and it is rare for teams to underperform or overperform their expected winning percentage by more than ten games. When that happens, is it pure luck? Is it the team's performance in one-run games? Is it the presence of a spectacular bullpen or closer? Is it clutch hitting? Theories abound, but compelling explanations are elusive.

The notion of expected winning percentage has caught on in other sports, each having a different exponent. In basketball, the exponent is much higher (somewhere between 14 and 17), while in football, it is about 2.4.[3] Nevertheless, an analytic explanation of why James's model was so successful eluded researchers until 2005, when Steven Miller proved that James's model, with an unknown exponent, could be derived by assuming that a team's runs scored and runs allowed were independent, and each followed a well-known statistical distribution.[4]

The fact that James's expected winning percentage hewed so closely to a team's actual winning percentage over the course of the season gave the A's confidence that they could accurately predict the team's likely finish once they had a good enough estimate of the strength of their offense relative to their defense.[5] We proceed with a discussion of how current sabermetric thinking may have led to DePodesta's estimates of those two quantities.

Offense

Clearly, the only quantity that really matters when evaluating a team's offense is the number of runs that they score. How they score those runs is a matter of taste, and the success of James's model for expected winning percentage over the course of the season might even diminish the importance of the distribution of *when* they are scored. Offense in baseball can be divided broadly into two skills: hitting and baserunning.

Baserunning

While baserunning is important, its value relative to hitting is small. Saber-metricians have estimated that most teams generally gain or lose at most 20 runs over the course of a season as a result of baserunning,[6] while individual baserunners rarely add or subtract more than 10 runs from what their team would likely have scored if they ran more conservatively.[7] Moreover, saber-metricians have suggested that even by creating a fantasy-style lineup of excellent baserunners, the upper limit on the value of baserunning is about ± 70 runs over the course of a season.[8] The average team scores and allows about 700 runs over a 162-game season, so the contribution of baserunning toward a team's offense is almost certainly less than 10 percent in practice.

Although some may view these results as dubious,[9] their credibility is aided by the fact that researchers have employed two entirely different methodologies and achieved corroborating results. The first empirical approach is to sum the changes in the expected run matrix (see Appendix for an illustration of how the expected run matrix works). That is, if there is a runner on first with one out, and if we ignore many particulars of the specific situation (who the pitcher and batter are, etc.), we can derive an estimate of how many runs are likely to be scored in the remainder of the inning. This estimate is likely to be about 0.5 runs. If the batter hits a single, then the runner necessarily advances to second base, and the number of expected runs increases to about 0.9 runs. However, if the baserunner advances all the way to third base on that single, then an additional 0.3 runs can be added to the expected run value. The empirical method for evaluating baserunning credits the runner with that 0.3 runs for each time he goes from first to third on a single. The reader can imagine any number of other scenarios in which a baserunner could be credited with taking the extra base. The fact that the myriad assumptions made are not actually true in each case is mitigated by the fact that we are primarily interested in how baserunners perform over entire seasons, giving us a sample large enough that many of those assumptions will be reasonable in an aggregate sense.

The second approach, which corroborates the findings of the first, is to build a simulation engine, and seed it with estimates of the probabilities of how often baserunners take the extra base. For example, one of the best baserunners in recent memory is Chase Utley, who, in addition to stealing about twelve bases per year while being caught less than 10 percent of the time, advances from first to third on a single roughly 45 percent of the time, compared to the league average of about 26 percent. If we simulate, say, one million innings of Phillies baseball with Utley running like he does, we get a good estimate of the average number of runs scored per inning for that team. But we can run the same simulation with Utley running at league-average rates, and compare the change in run scoring to the previous figure. The results suggest that even Utley's baserunning is worth no more than ten runs per season over that of an average runner.

Hitting

Like baserunning, the evaluation of hitters is complicated by the fact that teammates usually act in concert in order to push runners across the plate. For example, if the leadoff hitter walks, advances to third on a single by the second hitter, and then comes in to score on a sacrifice fly by the third hitter, then clearly all three players have contributed something to the scoring of that run. Conventional scorekeeping credits the leadoff hitter with a run scored (R), and the third hitter with a run batted in (RBI), but the second hitter is not directly credited for his contribution to that run. For this reason, sabermetricians have long lamented the focus on runs scored and RBIs in award voting, and sought a more accurate, balanced, and systematic way to credit each hitter for his contributions to run scoring.

One approach to doing this is to again sum the values of the changes in the expected run matrix. But this can be a complicated calculation that requires reams of detailed play-by-play data. A simpler, more accessible approach is to engineer a statistic that corresponds closely to run scoring for teams, and then apply that to individual players. For many years, it was assumed that batting average was the best way to do this. But while batting average does a decent job of explaining the variation in the number of runs that a team scores, it leaves much to be desired. In Figure 2, each dot represents one team in one season, and all team-seasons from 1954 to 2011 are represented (as in

Figure 1, each dot is slightly transparent, so that the appearance of a darker cluster indicates several overlaid dots). It is clear that as a team's batting average increases, the number of runs that they score also increases. Statisticians use a measurement called the correlation coefficient to describe the strength of that linear relationship. The correlation coefficient of 0.82 shown below suggests that about 67 percent (0.82 × 0.82) of the variation in runs scored is explained by batting average.[10] Thus, knowing a team's aggregate batting average (and nothing else) gives you a decent understanding of how many runs that team will score.

But there is a long way to go from 67 percent to 100 percent, and sabermetricians have sought to close that gap in inventive ways. One of the reasons that the A's focused so heavily on on-base percentage (OBP) in the *Moneyball* era was that it does a better job of predicting runs scored than batting

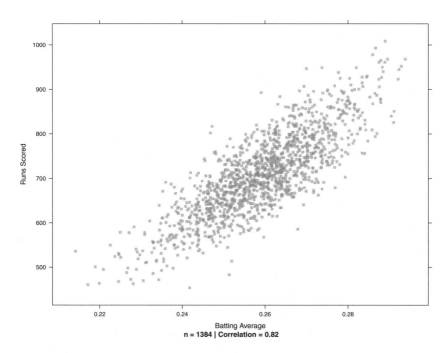

Figure 2. Team Runs Scored Versus Batting Average, 1954–2011
The relationship between a team's batting average over the course of a season and the number of runs that they score. The correlation is strong (0.82), but can we do better?

average. In Figure 3, the relationship between runs scored and OBP is more closely linear than it is for batting average, and the correlation coefficient is higher (0.88). Further improvements were made by OPS (the simple sum of OBP and slugging percentage [SLG]; its correlation with runs scored is about 0.95), which Lewis erroneously claims is "a much better indicator than any other offensive statistic of the number of runs a team would score."[11] In fact, it was known at that time that OPS was bested by a bevy of run estimators, most notably by Run Created, a nonlinear invention of James that in its simplest form is the *product* of OBP and SLG.

But suppose that rather than invent a formula out of thin air, you wanted to derive a formula based on simple assumptions about what the formula should look like. A common set of assumptions is that each offensive event

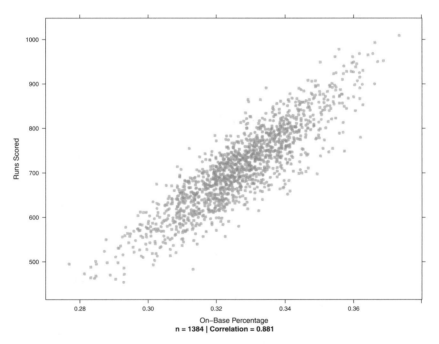

Figure 3. Team Runs Scored Versus On-Base Percentage, 1954–2011
The relationship between a team's on-base percentage (OBP) over the course of a season and the number of runs that they score. The correlation is stronger (0.88) than it is for batting average.

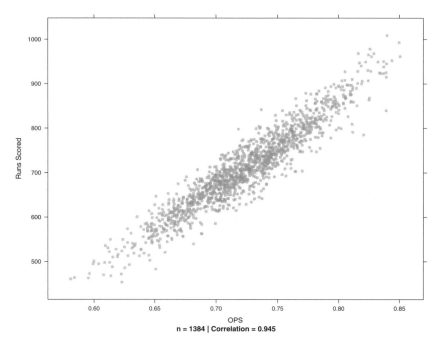

Figure 4. Team Runs Scored Versus OPS, 1954–2011
The relationship between a team's cumulative OPS over the course of a season and the number of runs that they score. The correlation is very strong (0.95).

should be associated with an average run value, and those run values should be summed based on their frequency. Clearly, a home run is worth, on average, more than one run—but how much more? Sabermetricians have devised two completely independent techniques for deriving these average run values, and arrived at similar answers. The first technique is to simply average the number of runs scored on each play. The second is to apply a well-known statistical technique called multiple regression using team statistics. It can be proven mathematically that the latter technique will provide the best fit to the data under a variety of assumptions. Thus, it represents essentially the best estimator that can be constructed with the idea that each batting event affects runs scoring in a linear fashion. Any run estimator that obeys these assumptions belongs to the class of linear weights formulas. While there are many linear weights formulas, we will use one known as eXtrapolated Runs

(XR).[12] In XR, a home run is worth 1.44 runs, and its correlation with runs scored is about 0.95.[13]

The value of OPS is that it provides a simple way to translate a player's hitting statistics into an estimator that we know corresponds closely to runs scored. Thus, knowing the OPS of each player gives us a better understanding of how many runs he is contributing to his team than if we knew only his batting average. Two players with identical batting averages could have significantly different OPSs, and we would be remiss in thinking that they were making equal contributions to their team's offense.

The popularity of OPS has much to do with its combination of simplicity and accuracy. Since it is the simple sum of two existing and commonly reported statistics (OBP and SLG), it can be computed in one's head quickly, and as we have shown above, provides a very good estimate of runs scored. The superior estimators outlined above are only slightly more accurate, but much more complicated to compute (try multiplying OBP and SLG in your head!). Nevertheless, since OBP and SLG are on different scales (the former is truly a percentage, the latter is not), the question of why the simple sum should be so accurate quickly arose. DePodesta supposedly found that by valuing a point of OBP at three times the value of a point of SLG, the fit to runs scored could be made even tighter.[14] Subsequent research has suggested that the true value is closer to 1.8, as opposed to three.[15] Nevertheless, DePodesta's calculation presented Beane with evidence that OBP was even more important relative to power than sabermetricians thought. This discrepancy made DePodesta's argument "heresy," which Beane interpreted as "good," and the "best argument he had heard in a long time."[16] It is implied that DePodesta's calculation was the primary motivation behind the A's emphasis on OBP.

Predictive Analytics

The preceding argument should make it clear that some of the more recent sabermetric hitting statistics (e.g., OPS, Runs Created, linear weights) are quantifiably better at estimating the number of runs that a team will score than older statistics such as batting average. Thus, it stands to reason that when applied to an individual hitter, they do a better job of quantifying his contribution to his team's offense. This captures the notion of the *accuracy* of the statistic. A separate but perhaps equally important question is whether those statistics do a better job of predicting that hitter's *future* performance.

To summarize, we now know that if one wants to estimate a player's offensive contribution, one is better off knowing that hitter's OPS as opposed to his batting average. The next question is, if one wants to predict a hitter's OPS next season, what statistic is most helpful? The answer is not obvious, and, as we will illustrate below, it is not as simple as knowing his OPS this season.

Forecasting the future performance of baseball players is a task that falls under the umbrella of "predictive analytics," a term that is increasingly common in the data-driven world in which we live. The task, as Lewis suggests, is not unlike what many financial analysts do, and, in fact, Lewis (a former financier) describes DePodesta as "just the sort of person" who might otherwise find himself doing exactly that.[17] In order to predict the future performance of baseball players, one needs a model that separates the elements of baseball that are predictable from those that are not. For clarity of exposition, let's call the former "skills," and the latter "luck," "chance," or "randomness." (In Nate Silver's parlance, these are the "signal" and the "noise.")[18] Randomness is by definition unpredictable (despite the best efforts of those financial wizards performing "technical analysis"). It is hopeless to try to predict the outcome of a random process, but what one can do is attempt to understand the distribution of that randomness, and conversely focus one's efforts on predicting skills accurately. This requires a nuanced understanding of what various baseball statistics actually reflect. Are they measuring skills? Or just luck? Or (as is most often the case) some combination of both? How much of each?

Every game exists on a spectrum that describes the amount of chance inherent to it. Some games, like chess, are entirely skill-based and involve no element of chance. Others, like the lottery, are completely based on luck and admit no skill. Baseball is a game that lies somewhere in between. Clearly, tremendous skills are required to play the game at the major league level, and players who are more skilled perform better over a long period of time. But chance also plays a large role, as the outcomes of games, and even championship seasons, can be determined by the tiniest unpredictable element (think Jeffrey Maier, Bernie Carbo, Bill Buckner, etc.). The same is true of statistics like OPS and batting average, which obviously capture the skills of different hitters to some extent, but just as obviously measure outcomes that have little to do with the hitter (e.g., the bloop single that happened to fall in for a hit). As in the game itself, it is not always obvious how much of what these statistics are capturing is skill, and how much is chance.

The notion of *reliability* helps statisticians distinguish between the signal (skills) and the noise (chance) present in a measurement. That is, if a measurement (e.g., batting average) is actually measuring something that tends to stay the same (e.g., a skill of a particular player), then repeated measurements should also tend to stay the same. Conversely, if what was being measured was actually due to chance, then one would expect to get wildly different measurements. For example, the height of an adult can be considered the ultimate skill, in the sense that it does not change (much or at all) over time, so repeated measurements of one's height are very likely to be the same again and again and again. Conversely, the number of five-dollar bills that one has in one's pocket is not a reliable measurement of an attribute of that person, because the quantity will fluctuate significantly depending on what one is doing and the change one received after one's last cash transaction. While attributes of people clearly do change over time (height changes rather slowly or not at all; weight changes more frequently), we expect that attributes of people are likely to be similar over short periods of time. Thus, if a statistic, when applied to the same player, remains similar over time, it provides evidence that what is actually being measured by that statistic is an attribute of that player. On the other hand, if we observe the statistic fluctuating appreciably over a short period of time, then it suggests that either what the statistic is measuring is not really an attribute of that player, or the attribute itself has little predictive value.

One technique for quantifying this notion of reliability is to examine the autocorrelation of the statistic. That is, to measure how the statistic changes with respect to previous instances of itself. In Figure 5, we show the autocorrelation of batting average for all batters with at least 250 plate appearances in two consecutive seasons during 1985–2011. Each dot represents one player in two consecutive seasons, with the horizontal coordinate representing his batting average in one season, and the vertical coordinate representing his batting average in the next

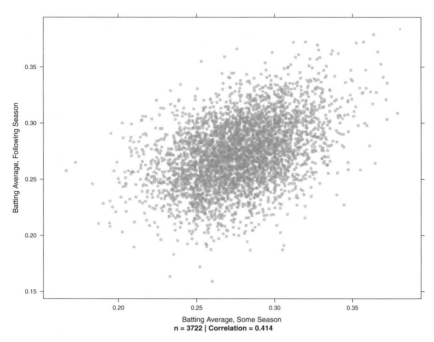

Figure 5. Batting Average, Batters
Batting average for batters exhibits a relatively low autocorrelation, mitigating its predic-
tive value and suggesting that it measures a great deal of chance along with batter skill.
Here at least 250 plate appearances in each season are required.

season. If batting average truly measured an absolute skill (like height), then we
would expect both coordinates to be about the same for each dot, and so the
points would be arrayed in a diagonal pattern, and the correlation coefficient
would be close to 1.[19] This would indicate a high reliability for batting average.
Instead, we see a pattern with a great deal of variation, and a fairly low correlation
(0.414). This suggests that knowing a player's batting average in one season does
not give a forecaster a very good idea of what it will be in the following season—
or more precisely, last year's batting average explains only 17.1 percent (= 0.414 ×
0.414) of the variation in a player's batting average next year.

Table 3. Properties of Batting Statistics

Statistic	Reliability[a] (year-to-year autocorrelation)	Accuracy[b] (correlation to team runs scored)
Strikeout rate	0.838	0.094
Walk rate	0.767[c]	0.422
Isolated Power[d]	0.739	0.805
Strikeout-to-Walk Ratio	0.654	-0.201
Slugging Percentage	0.620	0.910
eXtrapolated Runs per 27 Outs[e]	0.614	0.948
OPS	0.571	0.946
wOBA	0.570	0.942
On-Base Percentage	0.530	0.885
Batting Average	0.414	0.822
Batting Average on Balls in Play[f]	0.338	0.691

[a] We define reliability as the (Pearson product-moment) correlation coefficient between two vectors of data, where each pair is the value of the statistic in question in season x and season $x + 1$ for the same batter, provided that he had at least 250 plate appearances in both seasons, and that x is between 1995 and 2011. There were 3,722 such paired seasons.

[b] We define accuracy here as the correlation coefficient between the actual number of runs that a team scored in a season, and the aggregate statistic in question for the whole team over the whole season. All team-seasons from 1954–2011 are included.

[c] The relatively high reliability of walk rate was likely known to DePodesta in 2002, and is referred to indirectly by Lewis in his discussion of the A's acquisition of David Justice (*Moneyball*, pp. 150–151).

[d] Isolated Power is roughly the difference between slugging percentage and batting average, literally (2B + 3B + 3*HR)/AB or, sometimes (2B + 2*3B + 3*HR)/AB. The goal is to measure extra-base power, but remove the impact of singles, and usually to assume that doubles and triples reflect power equally, since the difference between the two is usually not so much how hard the ball was hit, but either the angle the ball was hit or how fleet afoot the batter was.

[e] As mentioned previously, eXtrapolated Runs per 27 Outs (XR27) is a linear weights formula. Its definition is XR = (.50 × 1B) + (.72 × 2B) + (1.04 × 3B) + (1.44 × HR) + (.34 × (HP+TBB–IBB)) + (.25 × IBB)+ (.18 × SB) + (−.32 × CS) + (−.090 × (AB – H – K)) + (−.098 x K)+ (−.37 × GIDP) + (.37 x SF) + (.04 × SH), and then XR27 = XR / (27 * (AB – H + GIDP + SF + SH + CS)). To clarify, XR is measured in runs; XR27 is runs per 27 outs. The idea of XR27 is to estimate the number of runs a team would score per game, if it were composed of 27 clones of one player.

[f] We define BABIP as (H – HR) / BIP, where BIP is balls in play. This includes all plate appearances that do not end in a home run, strikeout, walk, or hit batsman.

Mercifully, not every statistic suffers from low reliability. In fact, the rates at which batters strike out, walk, and hit home runs are much more reliable. As a result, it is relatively easy to predict how often a batter will do each of these things in the future, since simply assuming that he will repeat the previous year's performance is likely to be a good estimate. In Table 3, we show autocorrelations for many commonly used statistics, alongside the correlation with team runs scored. Note that statistics that are accurate (like OPS and SLG), in terms of the strength of their respective correlation with a team's runs scored, are not necessarily reliable, in the sense of being highly correlated with themselves over time. Thus, knowing a player's OPS gives us a good sense of how much he contributed to his team's offense in a given season, but it doesn't reveal all that much about what he is likely to do next season. Conversely, knowing a player's strikeout rate in one season gives us a good sense

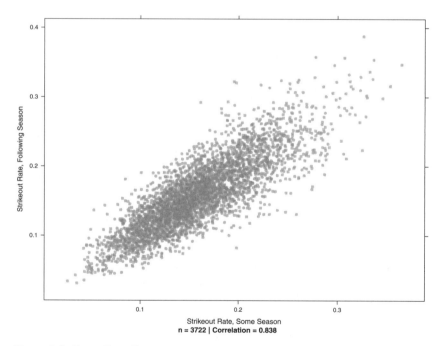

Figure 6. Strikeout Rate, Batters
Strikeout rate for batters exhibits a relatively high autocorrelation. This makes it quite predictable and suggests that it truly measures an attribute of a batter.

of what that player's strikeout rate will be in the next season (see Figure 6), but it is a poor measure of his overall performance.

It is natural at this point to question whether the high reliability of strikeout rate is of any practical significance. Since its paltry accuracy suggests that it is not a good measure of overall performance, why should we care what a player's strikeout rate is? One answer is that hitting is a zero-sum game, in the sense that there are only so many outcomes. Thus, if a player's strikeout rate is very high, that leaves less room for other, more desirable outcomes of his plate appearances.[20] At a certain point, it becomes extremely difficult for him to be productive, since his production is throttled by a high strikeout rate. For example, there have been only five players in major league history who have had a strikeout rate of at least 30 percent in two thousand or more career plate appearances.[21] All five hit for power, and four of the five walked at a high rate, so, for the most part, each was doing all he could do to compensate for his high strikeout rate. But none managed a .250 batting average, only one managed an OBP above .333 (typically the league average is around here), and none managed an OPS above .815, which is about what you would expect from a power hitter. The point is that although we might not care about a hitter's strikeout rate on its own, because the sum of all of his rates is one, and the strikeout rate is easy to predict, it provides an upper bound on the hitter's potential production. Twenty times, a player has qualified for the batting title (by having sufficient plate appearances) in a season in which he struck out in 30 percent of his plate appearances, but in none of those seasons did that player hit .300. It has never happened because to do so would require an astronomical batting average on balls in play (BABIP).

In Figure 7, we depict the most common outcomes of a plate appearance (PA) in the form of a tree diagram, with the relative frequencies of events indicated by the area of the circle containing each event. If the circle representing strikeouts gets bigger, then at least one of the other circles *must* get smaller. For reasons that will become clear later on, we have chosen to first separate all outcomes into either balls in play (BIP), or balls not in play (BNIP), where a home run is considered not in play, since in almost all cases, no fielder has a chance to make a play on ball that is hit for a home run.[22] It is possible to write the formulas for batting average and on-base percentage almost entirely as a function of the four quantities shown in gray in Figure 7 home runs, strikeouts, and walks per plate appearance (HR/PA, SO/PA, and

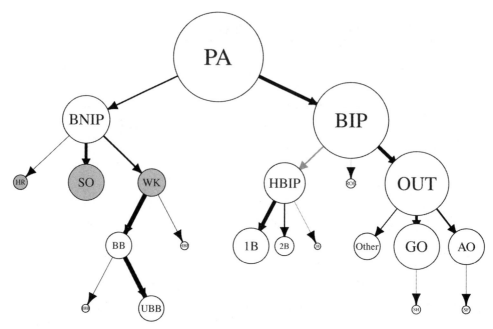

Figure 7. Tree Diagram Depicting the Outcomes of a Plate Appearance
The area of each node is proportional to the overall frequency with which it occurs, on average. The width of each edge is proportional to its relative frequency with respect to its parent event.
Note: WK is all walks and hit-by-pitches, accumulated since walks and hit-by-pitches have exactly the same effect. UBB are unintentional walks. HBIP is "hits on balls in play," so the critical BABIP ratio is HBIP/BIP. The OUT circle simply captures all nonhits on balls in play, with GO and AO representing ground outs and air outs, respectively.

WK/PA, respectively), and batting average on balls in play (BABIP).[23] Thus, in order to predict future values of batting average and OBP, one only needs to have estimates of those four quantities. Felicitously, we can see from Table 3 that the three quantities for which the ball is not in play (HR, SO, WK) typically demonstrate high reliability, making them relatively easy to predict. Unfortunately, the fourth quantity (BABIP) has the lowest reliability of any of the batting statistics we listed, making it difficult to predict accurately. Moreover, because the ball is put into play about 70 percent of the time on average, batting average on balls in play makes up a disproportionate share of the outcomes, and thus has a tremendous influence on hitting production.

With this perspective, the major difficulty in predicting a hitter's future performance is estimating his batting average on balls in play, since estimating the three other quantities can be done, for example, by simply taking a weighted average of the three most recent years, and incorporating the effects of player age and ballpark.[24] Due to its low reliability, this approach will not be very effective with BABIP. To the best of our knowledge, research that provides a significantly better way to predict BABIP either does not exist or has not been released to the public.

The idea that the reliability of a statistic affects its predictive value has been incorporated into many different models of hitting. It is often couched as *regression to the mean*, a longstanding statistical phenomenon that governs the behavior of random variables. Briefly, there is always a nonzero probability that random variables will take on unlikely values. But the likelihood of doing so repeatedly is, by definition, much smaller. Thus, unlikely observations appear to regress toward the expected value (i.e., the mean) upon repeated measurement in the future. For instance, if a player has an OBP of .370 in 2012 and the mean OBP is .333, then we would expect his OBP in 2013 to be somewhere between .333 and .370. Applications of regression to the mean in sports are copious, encompassing both the sophomore slump and the *Sports Illustrated* cover jinx, among other memes.

Regression to the mean is fundamental to virtually every well-known projection system, since it tends to reduce the error in future predictions. However, the question of *how* one should employ regression to the mean remains open. Typically, projection systems work by blending two relevant estimates of a hitter's future performance: the estimate concocted for the player by the system; and the league average value of that statistic. The final estimate of the future statistic for that player will then be a weighted average of the estimate generated for him, and the league average. This averaging regresses the estimate for the player toward the mean. But by how much?

In Tom Tango's Marcel projection system,[25] regression to the mean is incorporated via a function of how many plate appearances a player had in each of the previous three seasons. So to arrive at the estimate for Albert Pujols's batting average in 2004, you would combine a weighted average of his batting average over the three previous seasons (about .336), with a weighted average of the batting average for all position players over that same time span (.268), according to a weight (about 0.87) based on the number of plate appearances that Pujols had. The result (.328) reflects your belief in the observations you have made about Pujols's hitting ability, but also your knowledge of the hitting ability of position players as a whole. These ad hoc notions can also be formalized and refined into the language of Bayesian statistics, where a prior belief about the population (i.e., hitting ability of all position players) is combined with observations about a specific player (i.e., Pujols) via techniques that have been proven to be optimal under certain assumptions.[26]

Finally, any discussion about predictive analytics in baseball in the wake of *Moneyball* would be remiss without mention of its most successful applicator. Nate Silver, an erstwhile economic consultant at KPMG, sold his projection system PECOTA to Baseball Prospectus in 2003, the year *Moneyball* was published. As we have detailed Chapter 2, the success of Baseball Prospectus, which was in no small part due to the quality of PECOTA, gave Silver a venue for refining his predictive analytical skills. By the summer of 2008, Silver shifted those skills onto a new project: FiveThirtyEight.com, a website devoted to predicting the outcomes of national elections in the United States. After Silver correctly predicted the winner of the presidential election (encompassing correct predictions for the winner in forty-nine of the fifty states and the District of Columbia), as well as every U.S. Senate race, he received nationwide acclaim, a place for his blog on the *New York Times* website, and a two-book deal reportedly worth three-quarters of a million dollars.[27] One is left to wonder if any of this would have happened had Billy Beane turned Lewis away.

In summary, we have outlined the basic techniques for how sabermetricians analyze the two major components of offense: baserunning and hitting. We have developed the dual notions of accuracy and reliability, and explored the properties of many commonly used metrics in this light. With these dual notions come disparate purposes: statistics that are accurate are useful to quantify contributions in a given year, but not always useful for predicting future performance. Conversely, statistics that are reliable might not assess what we really want to know (e.g., their relationship to runs scored), but they might give us a better sense of what the future is likely to bring. In our view, understanding this distinction is critical to moving beyond senseless debates about, for example, whether the player with the most RBIs should win the MVP award.

4

An Overview of Current Sabermetric Thought II

Defense, WAR, and Strategy

In this chapter we first turn our attention to how sabermetricians have ap-
proached the analysis of defense in baseball and then focus on unresolved
issues in sabermetric thought. As we will see, for a variety of reasons, the
accurate measurement of player contributions on the defensive side has
proven far more elusive to sabermetricians than the corresponding offensive
components.

Defense

Bill James's model (and common sense) for expected winning percentage
makes it clear that preventing the opposing team from scoring is just as
important as scoring runs. The repeated refrain that "defense wins champi-
onships" is as prevalent in baseball as it is in other sports, although it is sometimes morphed into phrases like "good pitching beats good hitting." But the
concept of defense in baseball is more similar to that of soccer or hockey than
it is to basketball or football. In the former sports, one player (the goalie, or
pitcher) is designated almost entirely for defensive purposes, and he plays a
tremendous role in determining the number of points that are allowed, while
the majority of his teammates are often focused more on offense and play
more complementary defensive roles. Conversely, in basketball all players
must contribute on both offense and defense, and while some players may

excel in one facet of the game or another, there is no designation that changes what certain players are allowed to do. In football, with the days of the two-way player largely in the past, a change of possession usually brings a complete changeover of personnel for both teams. What is difficult in baseball (or soccer or hockey) is measuring the extent of the defensive contribution of the pitcher (goalie) relative to the other fielders (defensemen). In the same way that we presented separate discussions of baserunning and hitting (which together comprise offense) above, in what follows we present separate discussions of fielding and pitching (which together comprise defense).

Pitching

The evaluation of pitchers changed remarkably little until the theory of Defense Independent Pitching Statistics (DIPS) was advanced by Vörös Mc-Cracken in January 2001.[1] Prior to DIPS, starting pitchers were evaluated by their won-loss record, earned run average (ERA), and other proxies for the depth and quality of their contribution (innings pitched, strikeouts, etc.), while relievers were judged by those same metrics, but also saves and holds. Indeed, Bill James and Rob Neyer developed a simple formula to combine these elements into a Cy Young Predictor, which has correctly identified the winner of the Cy Young Award in sixty-seven of ninety cases since the award was first given to a pitcher in each league in 1967.[2]

Although many had noted how a pitcher's won-loss record depended heavily on factors that were entirely outside the pitcher's control (e.g., the offensive performance of his teammates, or the performance of the relievers who followed him in the game), ERA (earned run average) was still considered to be an accurate reflection of the quality of a pitcher's performance.[3] However, DIPS theory has largely discredited even this venerable metric, by demonstrating that the percentage of balls put into play against a particular pitcher that fall for hits is much more subject to chance than conventional wisdom allowed. Although the original incarnation of DIPS theory—that pitchers had zero control over this ratio—has been weakened by several arguments, the general thrust that pitchers have far less control over the batting average on balls put in play against them than was previously believed, is widely accepted within the sabermetrics community inside and outside of the industry. This tenet is now fundamental to understanding the relationship between pitching and defense. Indeed, even major league pitchers such as Zack Greinke and Brandon McCarthy are known to be disciples of DIPS.[4] This represents a considerable change since *Moneyball*, at which time "Mc-Cracken's astonishing discovery about major league pitchers had no apparent effect on the management, or evaluation, of actual pitchers."[5]

Given its importance, we explore this notion in some detail below. McCracken's original conclusion was: "There is little if any difference among major-league pitchers in their ability to prevent hits on balls hit in the field of play."

What does this mean? Certainly it does not mean, as has been a common misinterpretation, that there are no meaningful differences among pitchers. Nor does it mean that all pitchers should be expected to give up the same number of hits per inning, or even hits per batter faced. McCracken is talking about batting average on balls in play (BABIP), which we defined above as the ratio of base hits to balls in play, and observing that it appears to be largely outside the pitcher's control. That is, once the ball has been put into play, it doesn't seem to matter all that much whether it was put into play against Roger Clemens or Roger Craig. In a mathematical sense, McCracken's claim is that the conditional probability of a hit against each pitcher, *given that the ball has already been hit into play*, is more or less a constant. Thus, from a statistical point of view, there is little difference among pitchers in terms of their skill at preventing hits on balls in play. That is, if the league-average BABIP is about .290, then most pitchers do not seem to possess sufficient skill to keep their BABIP significantly and consistently under .290. However, the difficulty of putting the ball into play against a particular pitcher varies dramatically, and according to McCracken's theory, captures nearly all of the variation in pitcher skill. If this is true, then pitchers should be judged by what happens when the ball is *not* put into play against them; that is, by the number of strikeouts they record and the number of walks and home runs they yield.

The problem with a conventional metric, such as ERA, is that it depends heavily upon how many hits a pitcher allows, which, in turn, depends on his

BABIP, which does not appear to have much to do with him. Compounding the problem is that for most pitchers, the ball is very often in play. In general, about 70 percent of all plate appearances end with the ball being put into play, and, thus, if McCracken is to be believed, the outcome of about 70 percent of the plate appearances has little to do with the skill of the pitcher. Intuitively, this suggests that about 70 percent of a typical pitcher's ERA might just be noise, making it a relatively poor metric for evaluating pitchers.

One of McCracken's original observations is that great pitchers like Pedro Martinez and Greg Maddux ranked among the league's best pitchers in BABIP one year, but then among the very worst the next.[6] Does it make sense that if BABIP truly reflected a skill, that these two masters would suddenly lose, and then regain, that skill overnight? Would your answer change if the question were about strikeout rate? That is, would you believe that Martinez or Maddux would have among the league's highest strikeout rate in one season, and then among the lowest in the next?

These questions return us to the notion of the reliability of a statistic, and our belief that if a statistic is truly measuring a skill, then repeated measurements over a relatively short period of time should be similar. McCracken found evidence that this is not true of BABIP for pitchers. In our framework, we can quantify this by saying that the reliability of BABIP for pitchers is extremely low ($R = 0.17$, on a year-to-year basis), which we can see graphically in Figure 8. While the correlation is not zero, it is very low compared to other performance metrics, and the implication is that what BABIP measures is not so much a skill of the pitcher, but rather a combination of things that don't seem to stay the same for a particular pitcher. Clearly, the quality of the fielders playing behind the pitcher plays a role in determining his BABIP. The configuration of the ballpark (e.g., height and distance of outfield walls, extent of foul territory) plays a role. And chance plays a role, but none of these things has much to do with the pitcher. Accordingly, we observe that BABIP fluctuates from year to year in a pattern that is not consistent with complete randomness (because some of those things *do* stay the same over time, and pitcher skill *does* play a role), but is consistent with a large amount of randomness—which is far more randomness that many people were willing to concede.

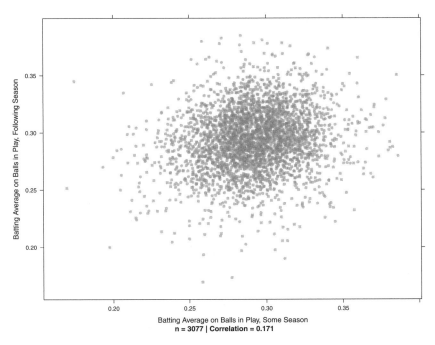

Figure 8. Batting Average on Ball in Play for Pitchers Has Very Low Reliability

Conversely, statistics that measure what happens when the ball is not in play show much higher reliability. As it did for batters, strikeout rate shows the highest reliability (R = 0.759), which is why you don't see great pitchers like Martinez or Maddux putting up low strikeout rates in their prime. This is because the percentage of batters that a pitcher strikes out has almost entirely to do with the skills of that pitcher, and while those skills may erode over time, they are not likely to change much from one season to the next. Similarly, a pitcher's walk rate is relatively reliable, since it too depends almost entirely on the pitcher, and reflects a persistent skill (his control) that is unlikely to change over short periods of time.

In the discussion of predictive analytics above, we suggested that a better model for predicting BABIP for batters would be an important step forward in predicting the future performance of hitters. The same is true of pitchers, and in our view this represents something of a "holy grail" of baseball analytics.

Table 4. Properties of Pitching Statistics

Statistic	Reliability (batters) (year-to-year autocorrelation)	Reliability (pitchers) (year-to-year autocorrelation)[a]	Accuracy (correlation to team runs scored)
Strikeout Rate	0.838	0.759	0.094
Walk Rate	0.767	0.629	0.422
Home Run Rate	0.740	0.318	0.717
Isolated Power	0.739	0.392	0.805
Strikeout-to-Walk Ratio	0.654	0.586	-0.201
Slugging Percentage	0.620	0.444	0.910
eXtrapolated Runs per 27 Outs	0.614	0.393	0.948
OPS	0.571	0.430	0.946
wOBA	0.570	0.448	0.942
On-Base Percentage	0.523	0.416	0.885
Batting Average	0.414	0.471	0.822
Batting Average on Balls in Play	0.338	0.171	0.691

[a] There were 3,077 pitchers who met the same criteria listed above for batters.

The search for a better way to predict BABIP began with McCracken's statement that pitchers had little or no control over BABIP, which implies that the best estimate of a pitcher's future BABIP is the league-average BABIP. Recall that in the discussion of forecasting models we presented above, regression to the mean leads most models to predict the future value of a statistic by forming a weighted average of the estimate of the player's ability with an estimate of the league average. The extent to which the first number is shifted toward the second number is different for every model, but it should reflect the size of the role of chance in the value of the statistic for a player. If the statistic measures pure chance, then the best estimate of every player's future statistic is the league average. Conversely, if the statistic measures pure skill, then you would use the individual player's estimate entirely, and discard the league average as irrelevant. The gauntlet that McCracken threw down implied that the best estimate of each pitcher's future BABIP was the league-average BABIP, or at least something very close to it.

The first major blow to this contention was delivered by Tom Tippett in

2003.[7] Tippett found that knuckleballers, as a group, had consistently lower BABIP than pitchers in general. Furthermore, he found that many pitchers with long, successful careers had consistently low BABIPs.[8] This suggests that pitch type plays a role in determining BABIP, and indeed this contention has stood up to further scrutiny. In addition, as we saw above, the rates of ground balls and fly balls put into play against a certain pitcher show high reliability, since they reflect attributes of that pitcher (e.g., his arm angle, the particular spin he puts on the ball, or the location of his pitches). The rate of BABIP on ground balls vs. fly balls is different, and thus it stands to reason that the rate at which a pitcher induces ground balls would affect his BABIP. This line of thinking has led to numerous attempts to improve the ability to predict future BABIP, but to our knowledge those improvements have been only incremental.[9] Controlling for ballpark characteristics also helps, but controlling for defense is difficult. In many ways we consider the future prediction of batting average on balls in play against pitchers to be the most prominent open problem in the field of baseball analytics.[10]

As the understanding of DIPS has permeated the sabermetric community, a plethora of alternative performance metrics for pitchers has been proposed. A clear evolution can be traced from Fielding Independent Pitching (FIP) and Expected Fielding Independent Pitching (xFIP), which ignore pitcher BABIP entirely, to Skill-Interactive ERA (SIERA), which incorporates additional variables like ground ball rate.[11] However, in our view none of these pitching metrics represents true insight into the relationship between pitching and defense in the way that McCracken's work did.

FIP and xFIP continue in the longstanding tradition of conjuring arbitrary constants so as to peg the scale of a new metric to that of an old one (ERA). But the scale of ERA is itself arbitrary, in that only runs have intrinsic meaning to baseball—earned runs largely reflect an outdated convention. What this field truly needs is a simple, illustrative, but effective model to evaluate pitchers. Until a model can be constructed with interpretable coefficients (*à la* linear weights), or with meaningful interaction of terms (*à la* Runs Created), no real insight will be gained, and there is unlikely to be any consensus about which metric is best.[12]

The statistical prediction of future pitcher performance thus boils down to two things that are relatively easy to predict (strikeout rate and walk rate), one thing that is hard to predict (BABIP), and one thing that is somewhere in between (home run rate). A more comprehensive approach—one that is employed by Nate Silver's PECOTA—is to pool pitchers into similar groups, and use the future performance of the group as a guide. Does the career path of a soft-tossing lefty like Jamie Moyer really have much to say about the career path of a big, strong, hard-throwing righty like Josh Johnson? Probably not, so it's probably more sensible to try to understand Johnson's career trajectory among pitchers who are similar to him in body type, repertoire, velocity, and so on (such as Curt Schilling and Josh Beckett). How those comparisons are made, and how the results are harvested, form the distinctions between prediction systems of this type.

Fielding

While much has changed in the decade following the publication of *Moneyball*, it remains true that there is no consensus about "exactly which part of defense [is] pitching and which part fielding, and no one [can] say exactly how important fielding [is]."[13] Nevertheless, as the theory behind DIPS has been refined and assimilated, interest in differentiating pitching from fielding has increased. In particular, many new metrics that attempt to evaluate fielders have sprung up and gained popularity, not only in the sabermetrics community, but also in the mainstream media.[14] We are not alone in remaining dissatisfied with these metrics, which have been likened to "a flashlight in a dark room."[15] In what follows, we illuminate the state of defensive metrics in a historical context, and provide a substantive critique of the limitations of the current state of the art.

Until play-by-play data became freely available on the Internet through the tireless efforts of Retrosheet and Project Scoresheet volunteers, attempts by the public to evaluate fielders in baseball were limited by the fact that only three basic statistics were commonly recorded: assists, errors, and put outs. Compounding the problem, the designation of an error was subjective, because it relied on the judgment of the home ballpark's official scorer—a human being whose objectivity, not to mention visual acuity, was often called into question. Fielding percentage (FPCT), which is simply the ratio of total plays made (assists + put outs) to recorded total opportunities (assists + put outs + errors), is a sensible way to combine those three statistics, and it remains the definitive measurement of defensive prowess for much of the baseball-watching world. But while the lack of objectivity that goes into fielding percentage is troubling, the question that FPCT addresses is not even really that interesting. It does provide a somewhat reasonable, if subjective, assessment of the relative sure-handedness of a fielder. But it says nothing about the at least equally important skill of range or the skill of leaping and timing. As Alan Schwarz points out in his excellent book, fielding percentage harkens back to the earliest days of baseball, when baseball gloves were little more than what Dan Marino might slip into the Christmas stockings of his offensive linemen, and the concept of an error referred literally to failing to catch a ball that hit you in the hands.[16] In today's game, the skill of sure-handedness or throwing accuracy is of questionable value compared to the skill of range, which measures how much ground a fielder can cover. Thus, the most important question is not "how often do you turn a ball into an out, given that it is hit to you?" but rather "how often do you turn a ball into an out?"

At this point it probably comes as no surprise that one person who popularized this distinction was Bill James. By the mid-1970s, James had created Range Factor (RF) to evaluate individual fielders, and Defensive Efficiency Rating (DER) to evaluate teams, using only conventionally available statistics. Range Factor measures the number of plays made by a particular fielder, which in theory quantifies the player's range. Unfortunately, this metric is of limited value when comparing different players, because the number of opportunities varies so widely based on a host of external factors, such as the composition of the team's pitching staff. Fielders who play behind a staff of strikeout pitchers are hopelessly uncompetitive with those who play behind a staff who "pitch to contact." Similarly, outfielders playing behind a fly ball–heavy pitching staff will have a leg up on those playing behind a staff of ground ball pitchers.

However, Defensive Efficiency Rating (DER) is the perfect complement to DIPS,[17] in that it is essentially 1 − BABIP.[18] That is, what percentage of the balls put into play against a team is converted into outs? In typical fashion,

James's statistic is both simple and insightful, and it directly addresses a not-immediately-obvious question of profound interest. But while DER may adequately measure the defensive performance of a team, there is no obvious way to apply the metric to individual fielders. Part of the problem is that the interaction among fielders is very difficult to disentangle. At the time *Moneyball* was written, a second problem was that "there wasn't the data available to make a meaningful appraisal of fielding."[19] Advances in the past decade may have begun to change that assessment.

Play-by-play data that is currently available from a variety of vendors provides much more detailed information, enabling more sophisticated models of defensive performance. Retrosheet data gives a zone that indicates where on the field a ball was caught, dropped in for a hit, or went through the infield (Figure 9). Proprietary data from STATS, Inc., Baseball Info Solutions, and Major League Baseball Advanced Media provide an even greater level of precision (or at least the illusion of it), by giving an (x,y)-coordinate pair over a grid of the field for that same information. Armed with this data, groups of researchers (many of whom are working for teams on proprietary models) have attempted to answer questions like: "If Derek Jeter is playing shortstop, and a ground ball is hit through the hole 22 degrees to the right of the third base line, what is the probability that he will turn it into an out?" It is important to note that, for the most part, these data sets contain no information about the spin on the ball, and only an ordinal description of the trajectory (e.g., ground ball, fly ball, line drive) and speed (e.g., hard-hit, medium, soft).

A non-exhaustive list of models known to the public that start with this question include ESPN's Zone Rating, David Pinto's Probabilistic Model of Range, John Dewan's Plus/Minus system, Shane Jensen's Spatial Aggregate Fielding Evaluation (SAFE), and the de facto industry standard, Mitchel Lichtman's Ultimate Zone Rating (UZR). While a full dissection of the differences among these metrics is beyond the scope of what we can accomplish here, they share a common mathematical core, which we discuss for illustrative purposes.[20]

Suppose that all balls hit into play can be divided into bins, in which all of the balls in the same bin are similar, in some sense. (The methodology for determining bins, and assigning balls to them, differs from metric to metric,

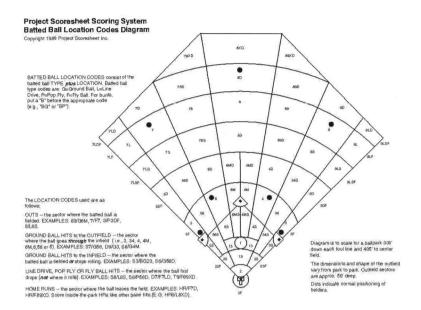

Figure 9. Project Scoresheet Hit Location Diagram

and from data set to data set.)[21] Then for each bin, we can estimate the probability that an average major league fielder at each of the nine defensive positions will successfully convert a ball in that bin into an out.[22] Moreover, we can estimate the average value (in runs) of a ball hit to each one of the bins. After all, a ball hit down the first-base line past the first baseman is more valuable than a ball hit through the hole between first and second, since it is more likely to become an extra-base hit. Finally, for each fielder, we have observations about each ball put into play while he was on the field, and which ones he successfully fielded.[23] By comparing his actual performance to his expected performance (based on the expectation of a league-average fielder at his position), we get an estimate of the defensive value (in runs) he provided relative to a league-average fielder. With the caveat that we have overlooked the details of this procedure, this is how UZR arrives at an estimate of the number of runs that a player has saved over the course of a season due to his range. The final estimate for UZR includes additional components for assessing throwing, sure-handedness, and the ability to turn a double play.

This is a start at a smart and reasonable methodology for evaluating fielders. So why are we so dissatisfied with the state of defensive metrics? Here is a non-exhaustive list:

1. UZR is a proprietary metric developed by a single person. Furthermore, the data that is fed into the system is proprietary. Thus, the system is a black box that spits out numbers in which we should have little confidence. For proprietary metrics of this nature, there is no assurance that the computation is mathematically sound, does not contain bugs, or even that the numbers are not simply picked out of a hat. The dangers of this state of affairs came into full view after the 2009 season, when Jason Bay's awful UZR numbers were "updated" by Lichtman.[24] Bay, who was considered by scouts to be an adequate, if unspectacular left fielder, was one of the worst outfielders in baseball upon replacing Manny Ramirez as the Red Sox left fielder, according to UZR. Meanwhile, Ramirez went from being a laughingstock to a slightly below average left fielder upon his trade to the Los Angeles Dodgers, who play in a park with a relatively large outfield, unlike the notoriously cramped Fenway Park. After Lichtman improved his ballpark estimates, Bay's UZR per 150 games of -13.8 runs was "updated" to +1.8 runs, transforming him from a lousy outfielder to an average one overnight, and during the offseason to boot.[25] Of course, this is nonsense, but we do not view the episode as reflecting especially poorly upon Lichtman. If anything, he should be praised for making improvements to his model, especially given the somewhat embarrassing light into which the changes were cast. Rather, the incident reflects poorly on all of those in the media and sabermetric community who tout the validity and accuracy of a closed-source, proprietary metric that is mysteriously controlled by one person. It seems hard to believe that Bay's imprecise UZR would not have been caught earlier had the formula for UZR been known to the public.

2. With the exception of the metric SAFE, no confidence intervals or standard errors for these estimates are provided; thus, the illusion of precision is perpetuated without quantification. Even stalwart proponents of UZR, such as Fangraphs' Dave Cameron, suggest that the margin of error is ± 5 runs per season.[26] This means, among all players from 2002 to 2011, almost 92 percent had a performance that was not distinguishable from zero at their position.[27]

3. While these data sets provide an (x,y)-coordinate indicating where the play was made, they provide no indication of where the fielder was standing when the play began. Thus, the separate skills of range and positioning are inherently conflated. That is, it is impossible to tell the difference between a fielder who actually covers a lot of ground once the ball is hit, and one who merely happens to position himself well before the ball is pitched, so that "what looked like superior defense might have been brilliant defensive positioning by the bench coach."[28] One might be tempted to argue that philosophically, we shouldn't care to distinguish between these two skills, since what is ultimately important is whether the ball is fielded, regardless of the method employed to do so. However, from a physiological standpoint it seems self-evident that range will decline with age, whereas positioning might not (in fact, it might improve), thus making the distinction important, inter alia, for forecasting purposes. Moreover, it is not even known whether positioning is in fact a skill. Further, the recent trend toward shifting infielders to the first-base side when left-handed sluggers are batting compounds the severity of this problem.[29] Finally, if the pitcher is successful in hitting the catcher's target, it simplifies player positioning and facilitates the jump a player gets on a batted ball.

4. It is assumed that the estimate of the probability of a ball in each bin being fielded is accurate, but in many cases this is probably not true. There is an inherent trade-off between making bins small enough so that all of the balls in them are actually similar, and having a sample size large enough to actually get a good estimate. Despite Lewis's claim that "any ball hit any place on a baseball field had been hit just that way thousands of times before,"[30] the truth is that (especially if one wants to make bins for each ballpark and control for batter and pitcher handedness), the sample sizes are much smaller, and the data only goes back to the mid-1990s at best. Furthermore, most data sets contain no information about the profoundly relevant issue of how long it took each ball to reach the designated (x,y)-coordinate on the field, or the spin on the ball, or the moisture on the grass, or the number of hops the ball took on its way there. In general, location is the dominant factor that determines into which bin a particular ball goes. Yet, a ground ball that goes up the middle in one second is clearly more difficult to field than one that takes

two seconds to get there. UZR employs ordinal data on three categories of how a ball is hit (slow, medium, fast) and two categories of the runner's speed (above and below average). This enables some consideration of these variables, but hardly allows for the precision that is often claimed or attributed to this metric.[31] Further, a player's range encompasses not only his side-to-side and back-and-forth mobility, but also his ability to leap and time his leaps; the latter skills appear to be left out of UZR, since infield line drives are excluded.

5. Again, with the exception of SAFE, the metrics presented above "could value only past performance."[32] The difference is that while the metrics in the methodology described above derive a model of the league-average fielder, and then measure the deviations from that model for individual fielders,[33] SAFE constructs a model of the individual fielder, using the league-average fielder as a guide,[34] and then evaluates the fielder based on the cumulative run value of the balls that he is expected to see in the future. This subtle distinction imbues SAFE with predictive inference that is not present in UZR.

6. The reliability of these defensive metrics is not particularly high. Yankee shortstop Derek Jeter notoriously scored poorly on UZR, on the claim that he moved slowly to his left. Then suddenly in 2009 Jeter's UZR rating, at thirty-five years of age, soared, placing him well above average. Outfielder Nate McLouth is another puzzle, with a UZR rating of −13.8 in 2008 but a +3.6 rating in 2009.[35] Jeter and McLouth are not isolated examples. Estimates of the year-to-year correlation for all players range from 0.35 to 0.45, which, as we saw above, is roughly akin to batting average, i.e., it is an unreliable predictor of future performance.[36]

7. Given the low reliability of these metrics, it has often been posited that three years' worth of data is needed to make an accurate assessment. The problem with this interpretation is that as the length of time over which data is collected increases, the assumption that the player's true defensive ability remains unchanged becomes less and less realistic. That is, it doesn't help to widen the time interval of study when the player is already changing within that window.[37] This makes estimating fielding ability somewhat of a moving target.

Many of these issues may be addressed in the coming years, when the long-rumored FIELDf/x data set arrives. FIELDf/x data, which is collected using a series of cameras mounted at the press level of each ballpark, promises to deliver exactly the variables that have thus far been lacking: the 3D position of the fielders and the ball at every fifteenth of a second during each play.[38] This has the potential to eliminate the concept of bins entirely, since now the probability of a ball being fielded successfully can be modeled as a continuous function of its position and the elapsed time that it takes it to reach a fielder.[39]

But while the never-before-seen data conveyed by FIELDf/x holds promise, not everyone remains convinced that it will lead directly to an accurate assessment of fielding. Bill James, for one, remains skeptical that FIELDf/x will usher in a new era of precise defensive evaluation. In an April 2010 interview, James opined: "We've had these cameras pointed at pitchers for several years now and we haven't really learned a damn thing that is useful. . . . I'd suspect the same thing would be true with respect to fielding."[40]

Another issue is that while it is taken as self-evident that important differences among fielders exist, it is not clear how important those differences are. In *Moneyball*, A's former statistical consultant Eric Walker is quoted as estimating that fielding is "at most five percent of the game."[41] DePodesta makes the more nuanced argument that "the variance between the best and worst fielders on the outcome of the game is a lot smaller than the variance between the best and worst hitters."[42] That is, DePodesta is skeptical that poor fielding cannot be overcome by good hitting. In other words, while the old adage is that "good pitching beats good hitting," DePodesta suggests that good hitting beats good fielding. Contrast this with the experience of the Tampa Bay Rays, whose last-place finish in 2007 was in part driven by their .669 DER, the worst in baseball history since the adoption of the 162-game schedule in 1961. Through various means, the Rays were able to improve their DER dramatically the following season, to a league-best .723. This led to a whopping 273 fewer runs allowed by the Rays, which fueled their first-place finish and World Series appearance. In many ways, the improvement in DER warrants the lion's share of the credit for the Rays transformation, since the team's offense actually scored 8 fewer runs in 2008, and the strikeout, walk, and home run rates of the team's pitching staff were largely unchanged.[43] Since 2008, the Rays have been able to sustain their defensive prowess, posting the league's best DER by a wide margin from 2008 to 2011.[44] The question of how the Rays achieved this remarkable transformation remains open to debate. In particular, it is unclear how large of a role defensive metrics like UZR played in the personnel changes the Rays made. Other factors may include position changes (e.g., permanently shifting B. J. Upton from the infield to center field) and an expanded use of defensive shifts. But, in any case, given the large number of runs allowed to be gained from a small change in DER, Walker, and by extension the A's at the time of *Moneyball*, most likely undervalued the importance of defense.[45] We shall return to consider the Rays sudden and surprising success in 2008 and after, and its relation to sabermetrics, in Chapter 7.

WAR

To this point, we have illustrated how sabermetricians estimate the offensive and defensive contributions of both position players and pitchers. In both cases, those estimates can be constructed so that they are on the scale of runs. A natural next step is to combine these elements into a measure of each player's overall contribution, whether offensive or defensive, in terms of runs. A final adjustment will translate runs into wins (using James's model for expected winning percentage), and the result is a statistic that measures how many additional wins each player contributes to his team. If we choose to interpret the size of this contribution in relation to a "replacement" level player, then the result is Wins Above Replacement (WAR).

For example, during the 2008 season, Fangraphs estimates that David Wright contributed 44.0 runs above average to the Mets through his hitting. As a baserunner, Wright cost the team 4.5 runs, while the value provided by his defensive contributions as a third baseman amounted to 5.1 runs. The sum of Wright's contributions was thus 44.6 runs above what an average player would produce. If a replacement level player, who is considerably worse than an average player, had played as often as Wright played in 2008, he would have been about 24.5 runs worse than average, so Wright is also credited with that amount. Finally, because Wright played third base, a more difficult defensive position than average, this provides additional value amounting to

2.3 runs. Thus, Wright is credited with 71.4 runs (44.6 + 24.5 + 2.3) to the Mets beyond what a replacement level player would have contributed. Since a quick-and-dirty estimate of the number of runs necessary to produce one additional win is about 10,[46] Fangraphs estimates that David Wright was worth about 7.1 wins above replacement to the Mets in 2008.[47]

The interpretation is that had Wright gone down with an injury in spring training, the Mets would have been forced to replace him. And if they did not have a major-league-ready prospect in the minor leagues, or another major leaguer on the roster who could play third, they would likely have to replace Wright with a so-called "4A" player.[48] This is a hypothetical journeyman who spends most of his time at the AAA level of the minor leagues and has success there. He probably has some major league time under his belt, but (at least recently) has not played a significant role for any major league team, and has not been able to hold on to a roster spot. Players like this are frequently minor league free agents at the end of the season and are assumed to be plentiful.[49] Thus, it is assumed that a player of this caliber is available to every major league team at any time, and his level of production represents essentially the worst-case scenario for the major league club. This is the Platonic ideal of a "replacement" level player.[50] A replacement-level player, by definition, contributes 0 WAR. Under the assumption that the Mets could have replaced Wright with a player (or group of players) who would have produced 0 WAR, the value that Wright provided to the Mets must be understood in relation to this level of production. In economic terms, what is being measured is Wright's marginal physical product.

While the idea behind WAR (modeling marginal physical product) is a good one, in our view the existing methodologies leave much to be desired. This is a shame, since the statistic appears to be easily understandable, which has enabled it to permeate the mainstream media.[51] Our concern is, in a manner analogous to the discussion of UZR, that the details of a statistic used by too many are known only to too few. Furthermore, there are some subtleties in the modeling aspect of WAR that may not be fully understood.

Currently, there are three popular implementations of WAR, one version computed and available through the Fangraphs website (known as fWAR), another version computed by Sean Forman and Sean Smith available on

Baseball-Reference.com (rWAR, sometimes also called bWAR), and yet another version available through Baseball Prospectus (WARP). As the three
sites do not use the same data set nor the same methodology, the numbers
returned by the three systems usually do not agree with one another.[52] For
example, in Table 5, we show the components that comprise the WAR calculation for David Wright's 2008 season from all three sources. While in this
case there is a general consensus that Wright was about a seven-win player
in 2008, there is considerable disagreement over the components that comprise that estimate. In particular, Baseball Prospectus viewed Wright as being
nearly 5 runs *below* average as a fielder, while Fangraphs had him at nearly 5
runs *above* average. In contrast, Baseball Prospectus viewed Wright's baserunning as having made a small positive contribution (1.5 runs), while Fangraphs saw it as being negative (-4.5 runs).

   This state of affairs is frustrating for anyone trying to understand the true
value of Wright's worth to the Mets. In part, the discrepancies among the
numbers spit out by the three systems speak to the difficulty of estimating
this unknown quantity. In effect, we have three different models, operating
on at least two different data sets, created by many people occasionally working together and occasionally in competition, all trying to estimate the same
unknown. What we would like to emphasize (and it is a subtlety generally

Table 5. Wins Above Replacement for David Wright in 2008

Source	Batting	Baserunning	Fielding	Replacement	Positional	RAR[a]	WAR
Fangraphs	44.0	-4.5	5.1	24.5	2.3	71.4	7.1
BB-Ref[b]	43	-1[c]	5	20	2	69	6.7
Baseball Prospectus[d]	49.4	1.5	-4.8	20.5	2.8	76.5	7.2

[a] RAR = Runs Above Replacement. Baseball Prospectus refers to this quantity as Value Over
Replacement Player (VORP).
[b] http://www.baseball-reference.com/players/w/wrighda03.shtml.
[c] Baseball-Reference includes a baserunning component and a double-play component, which
we have added together here to correspond more closely with the Fangraphs representation.
On the Baseball-Reference site, Wright is listed as having gained 1 run to his baserunning, but
lost 2 runs due to double plays.
[d] http://www.baseballprospectus.com/card/card.php?id=31514.

missed by the media) is that WAR is not a statistic akin to OBP or even UZR. Rather, it is an unknown quantity that is modeled more or less independently by at least three statistics (fWAR, rWAR, and WARP). While the creators of these models do generally recognize that the margin of error in their calculations is relatively large (± 0.5 wins by one estimate),[53] they do not provide standard errors or confidence intervals. Moreover, the overwhelming majority of players have WARs that are within one win of zero.[54]

What is needed at a minimum, in our view, to solidify the presence of WAR as a meaningful quantity worthy of discussion and comparison, is a fully open-source implementation of Wins Above Replacement. This would include:

1. A clear description of the methodology employed, preferably including mathematical notation and certainly including justifications for any arbitrary constants, scaling factors, or "corrections."
2. An open data set. At the moment this makes Retrosheet the only option, unless one is willing to parse the MLBAM GameDay files, and release the source code for that parser.[55]
3. The source code, using only open-source software, that will reproduce *all* of the calculations necessary to arrive at the final WAR estimates.[56]

The payoff to such an undertaking would be to lift the veil that obscures the details known only to the select few who stand to profit from the current implementations of WAR. Baseball Prospectus is a private company whose business model is predicated on subscriptions, so that readers can get the proprietary metrics that only BP provides. They can always claim that their implementation of WAR (e.g., WARP) is *better* than the open-source version (let's call it openWAR). Fangraphs and Mitchel Lichtman can always claim that UZR, a proprietary metric built on top of a proprietary data set, will provide superior defensive evaluations to the relatively crude estimates to which one might be limited by using only Retrosheet data. But at least when it is claimed that David Wright's openWAR in 2008 was 6.9 runs, with a 0.5 run margin of error, there will be universal agreement in what that number means, and what exactly went into the computation to arrive at it. Then, and only then, will it make sense for third-party organizations (e.g., ESPN or the MLB Network) to claim that Wright's WAR in 2008 "was" 6.9 runs. Under the current system, such a claim has no meaning.

As it stands, the problems with WAR have to do not only with the opaqueness of the underlying data and methodology, but also with known elements of the method that are dubious. For instance, a player's run differential is judged in reference to a replacement player, but it is not clear that there exists a pool of replacement players with the productivity that is ascribed to them.[57] Even accepting the run differential, the use of James's Pythagorean Expectation to convert runs into wins is less than robust. One need only reflect on the 2012 Baltimore Orioles, who outperformed their expected win total by 11 games, to see how inaccurate the runs to wins conversion can be.

Finally, many sabermetricians have taken the questionable WAR estimate and converted it into a marginal revenue product estimated via the metric MORP, or marginal value over replacement player. The basic idea here is to estimate the value of a player to a team and, thereby, inform the team how much it should be willing to pay the player.[58] To do this, an average value of a win is estimated at roughly $4 million and this average is then applied, with only the most minor of variations, to every player in MLB. As we show in Chapter 6, the value of a win varies significantly from team to team, depending on a team's win percentage, the economic size of its market, and other factors. Since MORP is intended as a guide to building a competitive roster, it makes little sense to abstract from profound differences among teams to estimate a player's value.

Strategies

The complexity of baseball is one of its great lures, and in the National League at least, strategic play continues to provide excitement night after night. Again, while many strategic maxims have become part of the conventional wisdom over decades of play, the more recent availability of play-by-play data has enabled sabermetricians to analyze these strategies with newfound precision. Although many baseball managers and fans are wedded to doing things by "the book" (e.g., sacrifice bunting), a new generation of thinkers has been more influenced by *The Book,* an ironically titled attempt to reconcile common knowledge with actual data.[59] Although some find the tone of *The Book* condescending, it ably covers important elements of baseball strategy in greater depth than we can achieve here. In a wide variety of publications, sabermetricians have tackled an ample array of questions, including platoon effects, lineup construction, reliever deployment, stealing, pitching rotations, intentional walks, base stealing, pitch selection, the hot hand, individual batter versus pitcher matchups, clutch hitting, sacrifice bunting, defensive shifts, and so on. In what follows, we will briefly characterize sabermetric thinking on a few of these topics, and illustrate common frameworks for thinking about how to address these issues.

Platoon Effects

It has long been observed that left-handed hitters have a much more difficult time hitting against left-handed pitchers, while right-handed hitters have a much harder time hitting against right-handed pitchers. Certainly, the angle of a pitcher's delivery is importantly different, and many hitters claim to "see the ball better" against a pitcher of the opposite hand. Most breaking pitches, such as the ubiquitous slider, break away from a hitter of the same hand, making them more difficult to hit. Indeed, since 1995 left-handed batters have hit nearly 60 points higher in OPS against right-handed pitchers (.782 versus .713), while right-handed hitters have hit about 42 points higher in OPS against left-handed pitchers (.773 versus .731). This discrepancy leads to the so-called "platoon" advantage. The strategy of attempting to maximize the number of plate appearances in which one's team has the platoon advantage has become de rigueur, and while its obsessive pursuit is often associated with Tony LaRussa, it was clearly known not only to John McGraw, the legendary New York Giants manager, but in fact to the earliest professional players. Bill James notes the presence of switch-hitters in 1871—the first season of what is now considered professional baseball—as proof.[60]

In general, hitters have the platoon advantage about 54 percent of the time, but managers can increase this percentage by matching effective platoon partners, using pinch-hitters off their bench, and having lots of switch-hitters at their disposal. Since 1995, the Mets have the distinction of fielding teams that enjoyed the platoon advantage most often (71 percent of the time in 2008, thanks to switch-hitters including Jose Reyes and Carlos Beltran) and least often (only 35 percent of the time in 2000, when they went to the World Series). Not only does the frequency of having the platoon advantage vary from team to team, but the size of the effect attributable to each player varies as well. A few players, like Jim Thome and Ryan Howard, put up Hall of Fame numbers against opposite-handed pitchers (1.058 and 1.020 OPS, respectively), but would struggle to start at their position against same-handed pitchers (.777 and .749 OPS, respectively). Conversely, a few players (Alex Rodriguez and Matt Holliday, to name two) have slightly better career numbers against same-handed pitchers. In this respect, sabermetrics has merely clarified, rather than turned on its head, the conventional wisdom about the advantages of platooning.

Clutch Hitting and the Hot Hand

One of the more controversial questions addressed by sabermetrics is about clutch hitting. The conventional wisdom has long held that certain players are "clutch" (such as Derek Jeter). The presence of clutchness imbues certain players with the ability to raise their game at the most critical juncture, often realized through a timely hit, a magnificent defensive play, or a biting third strike. A related (and often conflated) notion is that of the "hot hand," or streakiness. This is the suggestion that a player who is performing especially well is more likely to continue to play especially well. In some sense this is a weak converse to the notion of regression to the mean.

The problem is that statisticians have long doubted the presence, or at least the importance, of clutchness and streakiness. In the framework that we have developed in this chapter, a major flaw in the notions of clutchness and streakiness is that they do not appear to be persistent skills. That is, measures of clutchness and streakiness have very low reliability, suggesting that they capture more randomness than skill. In fact, the reliability of such metrics has been so low that sabermetricians began to question whether the effect was real at all. Bill James points to a seminal study conducted by Dick Cramer in 1977 that in the author's mind "established clearly that clutch hitting cannot be an important or a general phenomenon."[61] In an example from basketball, psychologists from Cornell and Stanford analyzed the shooting patterns of members of the Philadelphia 76ers in 1985 and found "no evidence for a positive correlation between the outcomes of successive shots."[62] Given the general interest in the subject, many researchers have tried and failed to identify incontrovertible proof that clutch hitting and/or streakiness exists.

But while many adherents of sabermetric dogma interpret this absence of evidence as evidence of absence, James smartly expressed skepticism in an enormously influential article entitled "Underestimating the Fog," shortly after the publication of *Moneyball*. James backtracks on several findings he had previously published and cautions his colleagues to embrace the limitations of their tools. Specifically, he warns against interpreting a failure to find evidence of an effect as evidence (or worse, proof) that said effect does not exist. From a statistician's point of view, this is like interpreting a failure to reject the null hypothesis as evidence in confirmation of the null hypothesis—an elementary misinterpretation. Among the more notable pronouncements James makes is that he believes clutch hitting to be an "open question," while "no one has made a compelling argument either in favor of or against the hot-hand phenomenon."[63]

We will leave the question of clutch hitting to the reader, but the question of streakiness has become an interesting episode in the history of sabermetrics. Since the world is generally far too complicated to model precisely on a computer (certainly this is true in baseball), statisticians create idealized models that behave nicely, and study those. A typical approach to addressing a question like streakiness goes like this:

1. Let's suppose (even though we know it isn't true) that all players behave like coins.
2. Let's flip a whole bunch of coins.
3. If the results from reality (the real players) are grossly out of whack with what was generated by the coin flips, then we can claim that the idealized model does not accurately capture reality. This may be

a finding, in that it implies that the idealized model, which does not include streakiness, is not sufficiently complex to generate the observations that we see in life. Conversely, if the idealized model (that doesn't include streakiness) describes reality well, then we haven't found evidence for streakiness (but we also can't say that it *doesn't* exist).

Using this general methodology, researchers at Cornell found that although Joe DiMaggio was an unlikely candidate to have a fifty-six-game hitting streak, there was nearly a 50 percent chance that *someone* would have had a hitting streak of at least that length over the course of baseball history.[64] Implicit in this methodology is the assumption that a player's likelihood of getting a hit is the same for each game. This is obviously not true in reality, but the results of the simulation suggest that the reality we have observed is a fairly likely outcome even if you do make this assumption.

In 2011, Trent McCotter pondered a more nuanced question: what happens if you switch the order of the games? In each game, each hitter either got a hit or didn't, but the games occurred in a certain order (i.e., chronological order). If streakiness exists, then you would expect to see more long streaks of games in which hitters got hits in reality than you would if you randomly reordered all of the games.[65] And McCotter found that in fact there *were* more such streaks, to a statistically significant degree.[66] McCotter interpreted his discovery as strong evidence that streakiness exists, and while there is still some debate about that interpretation,[67] it is clear that McCotter's work shows that the order of the games matters. This implies that players do go through longer phases in which they are more or less successful than randomness alone would predict. This finding would not have been possible even a few years prior, before Retrosheet provided the data and fast computers could perform the computations. Moreover, it is notable that the existence of streakiness has gone from self-evident conventional wisdom, to sabermetric anathema, back to some gray area where sabermetricians are grudgingly acknowledging its likely existence.

Sacrifice Bunting

One of the more quickly assimilated pearls of sabermetric wisdom was the avoidance of the sacrifice bunt. Many sabermetricians have written about the technique, generally finding it to be associated with a decrease in run scoring, rather than an increase. The argument usually harkened back to the expected run matrix (see the Appendix), which contains the number of runs an average team can expect to score in the remainder of an inning, given the configuration of the baserunners and the number of outs. Suppose we have a runner on first and nobody out. Then the expected number of runs scored in the remainder of the inning is about 0.87. If we successfully sacrifice bunt, then we have a runner on second and one out. But in this case the expected number of runs scored is only about 0.67, which suggests that our strategic ploy has cost us about one-fifth of a run.[68] In a competitive game, you simply cannot afford to give that away.

Or so went the thinking. By the mid- to late 2000s, sabermetrically oriented teams like Boston, Oakland, and Toronto eschewed the sacrifice bunt as a tool for generating offense, sacrifice bunting fewer than 20 times per season, or less than once per week. Conversely, the notably sabermetrically averse Colorado Rockies sacrificed 119 times in 2006, or nearly once per game.[69] Indeed, Oakland's bunting declined from about once every three games during the first half of Sandy Alderson's tenure, to about once every seven games in the five years following the publication of *Moneyball*. Interestingly, they have rebounded somewhat (about once every five games) over the past five years. Why might this change have occurred?

It turns out that while the initial observation that sacrifice bunting caused a decline in run expectation was not erroneous, it was foolish to extrapolate that the sacrifice bunt is always a bad play. For starters, the goal of maximizing expected runs is probably wise to pursue at the beginning and middle of the game, but toward the end of a close game, you are more likely to want to maximize the probability of scoring at least one run. Moreover, as the authors of *The Book* emphasize, the expected run values need to be put in context. The pitcher and batter are both rarely of league-average quality, so the calculation changes with each and every plate appearance.

Moreover, the manager doesn't get to choose to sacrifice bunt—he only has
the option to choose to *try* to sacrifice bunt. The consequences of failing to
sacrifice are varied, and usually even more harmful. And, of course, in the
National League the person usually sacrifice bunting is the pitcher, who
may be a far worse hitter, but a better bunter, a slower runner, a poorer
judge of the strike zone, and so on.

Here again, while the initial sabermetric insight was revolutionary, in that
it gave us a systematic way to analyze a strategy that had been in use for decades, it has been superseded years later by a more nuanced understanding
of the issue that is much closer to the conventional wisdom. This is not to say
that we have learned nothing, and certainly we are far better positioned to
make progress in the future, but it is unfortunate that the early adopters were
so vociferous that sabermetricians are now thought to believe things that they
no longer do.

Open (Hilbert) Problems

In 1900, the famed German mathematician David Hilbert published a list of
twenty-three unsolved problems in mathematics, which he considered to be
of particular importance. His list has been greatly influential to mathemati-
cians, who as of this writing, had resolved about half of the problems, and partially resolved another quarter. Among the remaining unresolved problems
is the Riemann hypothesis, which at this point is probably the most famous
unproven conjecture in all of mathematics. In 2004, before leaving Baseball
Prospectus to become the director of baseball research and analytics for the
Cleveland Indians, Keith Woolner published a list of twenty-three unresolved
questions in sabermetrics. While Woolner's list has been less influential than
Hilbert's, it covers a variety of topics that are of universal interest, including,
first and foremost, the question of "separating defense into pitching and fielding" discussed above.[70]

Woolner's Hilbert problems were separated into seven major categories:
defense, offense, pitching, developmental strategies, economics, strategic decisions, and tactical decisions. We solicited the opinions of a dozen or so of
the most prominent sabermetricians, to revisit Woolner's problems with the

benefit of ten additional years of research. While there is consensus on many subjects, confusion surrounds a few notable questions. Of course, each respondent has her own standard of proof, but the results hint at a divide between those in the public domain and those working for clubs.

Woolner's first problem, about separating pitching and defense, has probably attracted the most attention, and its placement on his list suggests that it may have been first on his mind at the outset. But while this question garnered interest among all whom we surveyed, some considered the problem to be still open while others thought it had been satisfactorily resolved. Mitchel Lichtman (in part due to UZR, but also John Dewan's qualitative identification of good and bad plays) believes that we already understand 90 percent of fielding and that FIELDf/x will give us the rest.[71] In contrast, Bill James, as we saw above, remains skeptical of this. Our own view is that, for reasons outlined above, there is still a tremendous amount of uncertainty surrounding the defensive evaluation of individual players. And while FIELDf/x will likely address some of the major unknowns in the current methodologies (e.g., the starting position of each fielder), it is hard to imagine that defensive evaluation will not be an active area of research for the foreseeable future.

Of equally general interest was Woolner's tenth problem: projecting minor league pitchers accurately. Here again, while Lichtman and Tom Tango consider this problem to be exceptionally difficult, one club official considered it "reasonably addressed." Lichtman hints at a potential reason for this discrepancy: "There is only so much you can do with the numbers. Of course insiders who 'know' or have access to people who 'know' these pitchers can or at least should do a lot better than an outsider who only has access to the numbers. Greater strides will and can be made in this area if and when front office analysts work more with the on-field personnel."[72]

Lichtman's larger point is that sabermetricians working for clubs are likely the only ones with access to critical information about the pitcher's repertoire, work ethic, mental discipline, health, and so on. The notion that sabermetrics and traditional player development information can be combined into analysis that helps not only the front office, but also the players, represents the current state-of-the-art philosophy. It is unfortunate, but perhaps inevitable, that lines of inquiry that were started by enthusiasts for the edification and enjoyment of a small community may be nearing their fascinating conclusion under lock and key.

Conclusion

The world that Michael Lewis presented in *Moneyball* contained a few brilliant members of the Oakland A's front office using their intelligence to outwit their competitors. Their strategy was based on sabermetrics, a discipline new to many, though it had originated roughly a century earlier and been cultivated by dozens of earnest collaborators. Without the implication that sabermetrics is real and works in practice, the *Moneyball* story might just be about an iconoclast who got lucky. But in the name of telling a good story, the details of sabermetric theory are sparse in the book and nonexistent in the movie. We have attempted in the last two chapters to rectify these oversights by presenting the basics of sabermetric thought in a coherent and accessible fashion.

5

The Moneyball Diaspora

Baseball was the first professional team sport in the United States. It was also the first sport to introduce collective bargaining and free agency in the players' market. And, it was the first sport to spawn the use of critical analytics to assess player performance and game and franchise business strategy.

The other team sports have always followed baseball, and the case with analytics is no different. Baseball, of course, lends itself to the use of statistical analysis to evaluate player performance, among other reasons, because it is easier to isolate the productivity of individual players in baseball.[1] This is true both because the success of a player depends directly on the actions of only one or two opposing players, and because there are a limited number of discrete outcomes from a play in baseball (as well as discrete possibilities leading up to a play). Hockey, basketball, soccer, and football plays are more interdependent and more continuous, and measurement of individual performance productivity is confounded by a host of complications.

Nonetheless, especially after the publication of *Moneyball*, the development of analytics in other team sports has accelerated. Interestingly, unlike in baseball, analytics practitioners in the other sports emerged roughly at the same time as the interest in analytics surfaced in team front offices. In baseball, the hobby of sabermetrics surfaced decades before the profession of sabermetrics. Thus, from the 1970s (or earlier) a growing group of intellectually curious stat heads began communicating with each other, trying to parse the myths and mysteries of the game. Later, in the 1990s, following the lead of

Sandy Alderson, Larry Lucchino, Dan Duquette, and others, the avocation of sabermetrics became the vocation of sabermetrics.

This succession in baseball meant that the first two decades of dialogue and insights occurred in broad daylight, in the public domain. In contrast, basketball and football analytics was quickly absorbed in the teams' front offices, and much of the statistical work in these sports has proceeded as proprietary, in the realm of commercial secrets.

Another obstacle has confronted statistical analysis in basketball and football. The best measure of performance is not total output, but total output per number of attempts, or efficiency. In baseball, measuring runs (or some other output) per inning is straightforward. In basketball or football, measuring points per possession is less so. In part this is because offense and defense can run together; that is, the ball can move in both directions on the same play.

According to some basketball metricians, settling on a consistent definition of a possession is necessary before a reliable measure of efficiency can be developed. So, for instance, if we want to determine the value of taking a shot in basketball, we must know both the number of points a successfully executed shot brings and the cost of either making or missing the shot (one leads to a change in possession and the other may lead to a change in possession). To know this, we must estimate the value of a possession—that is, how many points result from an average possession. But to know this, we first have to know how many possessions a team has in a game. This number is connected to the pace of the game and it is not as easy to quantify as one might imagine.

Let us assume that we can measure the number of possessions and that the average possession yields one point to the offensive team. In this case, when a player sinks a three-point shot, the shot gives the other team possession and, hence, one point on average. So, the expected net value of the three-point conversion is two points. (This observation is mitigated by the existence of the shot clock in professional basketball which mandates that the ball will change possession every twenty-four seconds, whether or not a shot is taken and/or made. Thus, a three-point shot at or near the buzzer does not really *cause* a change in possession.[2] Although there is no possession clock in football, football shares the characteristic with basketball that a score necessarily leads to a change in possession.) A similar netting out procedure would not have to be performed for a hit (or run) in baseball, because the hit (or run) does not bring that inning closer to an end. It would, however, have to be assessed in reference to an out.

Another thing that aids quantitative analysis in baseball is the large sample size. Teams play 162 regular season games per year, roughly twice the number in basketball and hockey, four times the number in soccer, and ten times the number in football. Therefore, most annual statistics in baseball necessarily experience less random fluctuation.[3]

In sum, because of (a) the less open nature of analytics outside baseball, (b) the greater statistical conundrums outside baseball, (c) the less discrete and more collective nature of football, basketball, hockey, and soccer, and (d) the smaller sample size for most statistics, the analytic insights from quantitative study in these sports are either more inchoate or more elusive.

The Spread of Analytics Outside Baseball

Similar to baseball, it is not a simple matter to identify when the application of critical statistical analysis of performance and strategy was first introduced into the front offices of football, basketball, or other sport teams. Some teams did hire statisticians decades ago, but whether these employees did more than assemble the basic box scores and maybe add a few tweaks, and how any of this information was put to use, is more difficult to discern.

For instance, the NBA's New York Knickerbockers hired Dave Heeren in 1961 as the team statistician. In 1958, Heeren had developed what he called the TENDEX formula for evaluating players.[4] In its initial version, a player's TENDEX rating equaled the sum of his points, rebounds, and assists, minus missed field goal attempts and missed free throw attempts. Heeren evolved the formula into more sophisticated versions over the years. TENDEX became the basis for the NBA Efficiency rating and for subsequent linear weights metrics of player and team performance. It is unclear, however, to what extent the Knicks or any other team made effective use of this rating system, and, as we shall see, the various incarnations of linear weights in basketball all have significant limitations.

Heeren did not begin to publish articles on his system until the late 1980s. He published his first TENDEX book in 1989. Dean Oliver, Bob Bellotti, and John Hollinger began writing in the 1990s, primarily on websites, suggesting various refinements and elaborations to TENDEX, as well as other evaluation methodologies. The proliferation of articles, books, and websites using quantitative analysis of basketball, however, did not begin until after 2000.

Also after 2000, NBA front offices began to embrace the notion that they could improve team performance by a more sophisticated application of statistical analysis. The practice of basketball analytics has evolved cautiously since then. Soon after he purchased the Dallas Mavericks in 2000, Mark Cuban hired decision sciences professor Wayne Winston, his former teacher at Indiana University, as a stats consultant. Cuban seems to have been first basketball owner to explore the application of analytics. Cuban's explanation for his innovative move is straightforward: "I wanted to give the Mavs any advantage that I possibly could."[5]

Upon finalizing his purchase of the Celtics in January 2003, Wyc Grousbeck hired Daryl Morey as vice president of strategy and information to do statistical analysis. Grousbeck's background was in biotech and software venture capital. He realized that the Celtics' front office was in dire need of overhaul and modernization, and he wanted to exploit every opportunity to give his team a leg up on the competition. One of the first statistical insights to benefit the Celtics was the discovery that twenty-four of the previous twenty-five NBA champions had three all-star players on their roster,[6] and, most important, one of the three was a league MVP or Top Fifty all-time player. Eventually this insight led to the Celtics' plan to get Kevin Garnett.

In October 2004, the Seattle SuperSonics hired Dean Oliver as a full-time quantitative analyst. In 2005, in preparation for the NBA draft, the Portland Trailblazers commissioned Protrade Sports (subsequently acquired by Yahoo) to develop a model to predict how college players would perform in the NBA based on drafted players over the previous ten years. In December 2005, Cleveland Cavaliers GM Danny Ferry hired Dan Rosenbaum as a statistical analyst. In April 2006, the Houston Rockets hired Daryl Morey as their assistant general manager and announced that Morey would become the general manager during the next season. During the 2009–10 season, Aaron

Barzilai, Alex Rucker, Ryan Parker, Jon Nichols, Kevin Pelton, and Ken Cata-
nella, all from various analytic websites, were hired to do statistical analysis
in the NBA. Interestingly, most of the hires were of people participating on
the APBRmetrics bulletin board.[7] After the hires, the activity on the board
diminished appreciably.[8]

And so it went, step by step. During the 2010–2011 season, Benjamin Alamar, founder of the *Journal of Quantitative Analysis in Sports* and team statistician for the Oklahoma City Thunder, estimated that roughly half of the
teams had a "metrician" working in their front office. And, prior to the beginning of the 2012–2013 season, Dean Oliver, now working as the director of
ESPN's analytics department, identified at least twenty-two NBA teams with
a metrician. Further, Oliver anticipated that two more teams were about to
add quantitative analysts.

In mid-December 2012, the new ownership group of the Memphis Griz-
zlies poached John Hollinger, best known for developing the comprehensive
Player Efficiency Rating, from ESPN to become its vice president of basketball operations. In his farewell column for ESPN, Hollinger offered the following assessment:

> It's hard to believe this is true, but just eight years ago very few teams
> showed any interest in analytics, and those who did wouldn't admit
> it publicly. Seriously. Teams employed analytics people they wouldn't
> even mention in their directory for fear of ridicule.
>
> In less than a decade, teams have reversed course: Now, if any-
> thing, many try to promote how much they're doing with analytics.
> At least two-thirds of the league's teams have invested in this area,
> and while a few of them are just checking a box, most are seriously
> committed to it.[9]

In professional football, owing primarily to the more continuous and interdependent nature of play and very sparse data, the incorporation of analytics into team front offices has been more halting. Nonetheless, basic statistical
analysis has been around for decades in the NFL. Bud Goode worked analyzing statistics for twenty-one different teams over the years and carried out

some rudimentary quantitative tests. He found, for instance, that yards per pass was the strongest predictor of team win percentage among a variety of game stats.

In 1971, an article co-authored by former Chicago Bears quarterback Virgil Carter in *Operations Research*, based on data from the first half of the 1969 season, plotted the net number of points scored when a team had a first down at different field positions. For instance, the article found that the net points on average when a series began on the team's own five-yard line was minus 1.2 points (i.e., the team on defense was more likely to score than the team on offense) and 6 points when the series began on the opponent's five-yard line. The relationship was pretty much linear between these two points. This article adumbrated a line of research that began in earnest with Bob Carroll and Pete Palmer's 1988 book, *The Hidden Game of Football*, and continued with David Romer's 2006 article that will be discussed below.[10]

Evaluating individual performance in football, however, has always been tricky. An individual's stats, whether completion percentage, yards per pass, yards per rush, interceptions, or tackles, depend heavily on the work of one's teammates. The outcome of a play in football is essentially the result of a matchup of eleven players against eleven players, whereas in baseball it is basically a one-on-one matchup. It is perhaps for this reason that practitioners of football metrics have yet to appear widely in NFL teams' organizational charts. The New Orleans Saints moved beyond the use of magnetic boards during the league-wide amateur draft to the use of a computer program that electronically depicted the draft's progression. The San Francisco 49ers hired Paraag Marathe, a Stanford MBA and former Bain Capital employee, to do statistical analysis back in 2000. Today, he is the team's COO and Brian Hampton does some work for the 49ers with analytics. The Philadelphia Eagles, New England Patriots, and Dallas Cowboys are also known to have put some emphasis on statistical analysis in making personnel and game strategy decisions. Further, prior to the 2012-2013 season the Jacksonville Jaguars and Baltimore Ravens (on the way to their Super Bowl victory) hired stat analysts.[11] And the Buffalo Bills announced in early 2013 that they are "going to create and establish a very robust football analytics operation that [is] layer[ed] into our entire operation moving forward."[12] But, beyond these examples, there is little evidence of widespread employment of analytics staff, let alone of the integration of analytics into decision-making, as a way to achieve competitive advantage in the NFL.[13]

The New England Patriots may be the exception that proves the rule. Although the details of the internal workings of the Patriots front office are proprietary, it appears as though the Patriots have been applying analytics to evaluate players and orchestrate roster management since 1994, when Robert Kraft bought the team from Jim Orthwein. Of course, 1994 was also the first year of the NFL salary cap and Jonathan Kraft, with his background in finance at Bain & Co., anticipated that cap management would become a key to team success. Together with his former workmate at Bain, Andy Wasynczuk, the Pats' front office began to build statistical models for valuing players and roster management. When Bill Belichick became the assistant head coach in 1996, the Pats were able to begin to integrate the on-field and front office practices, and then were able to build upon this when Belichick returned to the Patriots as head coach in 2000. Belichick not only brought superb coaching skills but also a keen intellect that was able to understand and not be threatened by the statistical approach of the team's front office. As time went on, Belichick integrated new game strategies based on statistical analysis. Unlike many coaches in professional sports, Belichick was willing to take heat from the media if he tried innovative game tactics and failed—knowing that the probabilities of success were on his side, even though his novel choices would not succeed every time. It is noteworthy that, notwithstanding Michael Lewis's interpretation that the Oakland A's around the turn of the century were the first team to marry new statistical analytical methods with the making of roster and strategy decisions, it appears that the Patriots may have beaten Billy Beane to the altar.

Basketball Analytics

Analytical work on individual basketball performance began with Dave Heeren's TENDEX system, as noted above. TENDEX was modified numerous times over the years, first dividing output by minutes played in the 1960s, then adding blocked shots, steals, and turnovers in the 1970s as the NBA began to tabulate these stats, among other elaborations. TENDEX became the basis for a variety of linear weights models, each adding or subtracting various basketball plays and weighting each according to their estimated contribution to scoring or net scoring.

The simplest adaptation of TENDEX was the NBA's own NBA Efficiency rating. The formula for NBA Efficiency (NBA-E) was:

NBA-E = points + rebounds + assists + steals + blocks – missed field goals – missed free throws – turnovers

Note that the formula gave equal weight to each of these actions. John Hollinger developed a variant known as PER (Player Evaluation Rating), and Dean Oliver brought more sophistication to the analysis by incorporating the concepts of possession and pace.

In order to understand the true efficiency of a player, it is necessary to know the cost as well as the benefit of his actions. As noted above, once possession was defined, it was possible to estimate the average points scored per possession and, hence, know the average cost of losing possession (e.g., a missed field goal shot or a turnover).[14] A player's total output is also affected by how many possessions a team has during a game, which, in turn, is determined by how fast the game is played (pace). Just as outs per team are equal in baseball, possessions per team are equal in basketball.

Despite the advances in the linear weights approach, David Berri has argued that most of the player and team performance models, by underweighting lost possession, have overvalued scoring, at the expense of other actions, such as rebounds, assists, or steals.[15] Berri has also observed that statistical models of player salaries overvalued scoring as well; that is, owners generally paid high scorers more than their actual contribution to team wins warranted.[16] Hence, Berri suggested the presence of a market inefficiency—that is, GMs could build cheaper and better teams by placing more priority on players' nonscoring attributes.[17]

While these linear weights models have improved our understanding of the game and of how to evaluate players, they also come up short in a number of ways. There are many elements of defensive performance that they do not capture, and they do not do justice to the interdependence of play: for instance, whether a player has a shot, and whether it is an easy or difficult shot, may depend on a good pick being set, a sharp assist being made, or poor defense being executed.

Accordingly, a more inclusive player evaluation approach was introduced. This approach, the plus/minus and adjusted plus/minus systems, was adapted from the plus/minus system in hockey. The plus/minus system in hockey simply records whether the team gained or lost net goals when a player was on the ice.[18] The system in basketball records the net gain or loss in points while a player is on the court. So, if the Miami Heat is behind 50-48 when LeBron James enters the game, but ahead 60-54 when he goes back to the bench, then James takes the team from down 2 to up 6, and he is credited with a +8 score for that period of play. By its nature, the plus/minus tally allows *all* events on the court to influence the recorded score attributed to the player and it does not have to be concerned with either identifying or weighting the various events.

One problem with the plus/minus system is that the presence of an individual player in the game may have no, little, or substantial impact on the score differential. Accordingly, the plus/minus model has been modified to account for the quality of the other players on the court—this is called the Adjusted Plus/Minus (APM). Even in this case, however, the synergy or lack thereof of a particular group of players will still influence a player's APM. Further, from the point of view of a GM or a coach, the APM or raw plus/minus system tells one little about how the specific skills that a player brings to the court influence the observed score differential. Finally, the APM value shows low reliability (i.e., low correlation for individual players from one year to the next);[19] endowing the metric with little predictive value and making it problematic to use as a guide to personnel decisions.

Since the linear weights and plus/minus systems have complementary strengths and weaknesses, it is not surprising that one of the new approaches is to combine them. For instance, the APM score for a player can be used as a dependent variable and regressed on the player's box score stats (points, shot percentage, assists, rebounds, etc.), yielding a result called Statistical Plus/Minus. While this approach may fill some holes by identifying the specific nature of a player's contribution, it does not fill them all.[20] Hence, analysts continue to experiment with other methods that endeavor to identify metrics regarding the interdependencies of team play.

Football Analytics

Similar to basketball, in football all the players on the field are likely to have an impact on every play. For instance, if an offensive guard misses a block, a pass play is likely to abort or a run is likely to fall short. This guard has an important role in virtually every offensive play.[21] This is in distinct contrast to baseball, where a batter is up maybe four times a game, which might amount to only 5 percent of the plays in the game. A baseball fielder (outside of the battery) might be involved in anywhere from zero to ten plays a game. Because football and basketball players can impact every play (allowing for the defense/offense platoon in football), each player can be more decisive in the determination of the game's outcome. But unlike in basketball, where there are only five players, football has twenty-two players plus two kickers (not counting special teams), so the importance of an individual player is bound to be smaller than in basketball.

In football, because all eleven players are probably contributing in some way to the success of the play and each player's execution cannot be precisely measured, there is a large issue with attribution. A running back depends on the blocks and blocking scheme of the linemen, the handoff (and fakes) from the quarterback, the defensive alignment and execution, the play call given the game situation, and so on. Every play has these interdependencies.

And there are other conundrums. For instance, after extensive study of video and interviews, the ESPN football analytics team attempted to allocate responsibility for a successful long pass. They began with the hunch that a long pass requires not only distance but precision from the quarterback and so a quarterback should receive more of the credit for a successful long pass than the end who caught it. Similarly, a short pass is easier to throw and harder to catch, so the receiver should get more of the credit. What they discovered is exactly the opposite. For most long passes, the receiver has to adapt to the throw, slowing down, speeding up, taking a different angle, repositioning himself vis-à-vis the defender. Most short passes demand speed, precision, and timing from the quarterback, whereas the receiver runs to a designated spot. One might question this finding, but the fact that all these variables are in play is hard to deny.

It is also hard to deny that some of the traditional metrics that have been used in football, such as the well-traveled NFL Passer Rating, are based on arbitrary elements and can be improved upon with careful thought and analysis.[22] Such modifications, elementary though they may be, can still provide a competitive advantage to teams that are willing to be open-minded about new metrics.

So, where does that leave football analytics? There are always new twists for player ratings systems and for evaluating game strategies.[23] One of the more prominent analyses of game strategy was published by University of California, Berkeley economist David Romer in 2006. Romer asked the questions: when should teams facing fourth down go for the first down, when should they attempt a field goal, and when should they punt? In order to answer these questions, Romer needed to generate a probability function of point outcomes at different yard lines for both the offensive and defensive teams. The analysis must assess the chances of making the necessary yardage for a first down or touchdown times the point value of success (e.g., seven points for a touchdown with extra point) and the expected value for the opponent if the team fails to get a first down or touchdown, given that the opponent will start a series at a particular yard line. In order to undertake this analysis, Romer generated a yardage chart (Figure 10).

Romer compared his model with actual team choices and concluded that coaches generally are too conservative on fourth down.[24] The risk-averse coaches seem to prefer making the call that is anticipated by football convention rather than the call that maximizes expected point value. The potential praise for being aggressive and right apparently is more than offset psychically by the scorn that would rain down on the coach if the aggressive play did not pan out. Romer's analysis has since been corroborated and extended by several studies.[25] Notable among the extensions is the work of Brian Burke at advancednflstats.com. Burke has elaborated the expected points based on field position model to include the down and yards to go, as well as adjustments for the game score.

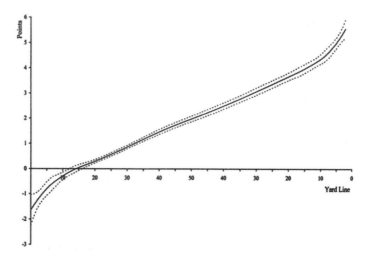

Figure 10. The Values of Situations
Source: David Romer, "Do Firms Maximize: Evidence from Professional Football," *Journal of Political Economy* 114 (2006): 346.

As suggested earlier, Bill Belichick appears to be the exception that proves the rule. In an important game against the Indianapolis Colts on November 15, 2009, Belichick's swagger got the best of him. Nursing a six-point lead with 2:08 to go, Belichick decided to go for it on fourth-and-2 from his own 28 instead of punting the ball and making Peyton Manning and the Indianapolis Colts go 80 yards for the score. The fourth-down play failed, the Colts took over possession and scored with ease, winning their ninth straight game (35–34) and getting in the driver's seat for home-field advantage in the AFC playoffs. Belichick was subsequently raked over the coals by commentators.

One indication of the difficulty in finding suitable football performance metrics is the lack of consistency in the major indicators. As discussed in Chapter 3, a reliable performance metric should have at least two qualities: a strong relationship with team wins and predictive ability. Predictive ability comes from year-to-year consistency. If a metric succeeds in explaining a high percentage of the variation in team wins, but it fails in that individual players do not have consistently high or low performance from one year to the next as measured by the indicator, then the metric will do little good to

GMs who are trying to put together a winning team. Using data from 1994 through 2007, David Berri and Martin Schmidt find the key football metrics have very low consistency.[26] For instance, the percent of variation in a metric in year two explained by variation in the metric in year one for major performance variables is as follows.[27]

For Quarterbacks:

Fumbles per play	3 percent
Yards per pass attempt	18 percent
Completion percentage	24 percent
Sacks per attempted pass	25 percent
Rushing yards per attempt	26 percent

For Running Backs:

Receiving yards per reception	1 percent
Fumbles lost per play	2 percent
Rushing yards per attempt	13 percent

Compare these statistics with some of those in basketball:

Field goal percentage	47 percent
Free throw percentage	59 percent
Field goal attempts per minute	75 percent
Points per minute	75 percent
Blocked shots per minute	87 percent
Assists per minute	87 percent
Rebounds per minute	90 percent

Or, with baseball:

OPS	43 percent
Strikeouts per nine innings	62 percent

Any new composite performance metric will be made up of these standard indicators. If the indicators vary widely from year to year for the same player (presumably, in part, because they depend heavily on one's teammates and opposing players), then they will not provide a reasonable basis for personnel decisions. In this regard, the low year-to-year correlations in football performance metrics stand out, and present a particularly difficult challenge to metricians seeking to identify more significant statistics.[28] Nonetheless, simple advances in some conventional statistics are attainable and may help teams get a leg up on the competition, as appears to have been true for the New England Patriots.

It is important to observe, however, that we have not directly traced the Patriots' on-field success to their use of new metrics or analytical modes. As with baseball, it appears that it is the most intelligent front offices that embrace new methods, especially new methods requiring specialized knowledge that the top executives may not possess, and the success of these teams may be a function of elements of front office intelligence that are not connected to statistical analysis.

Assessing the Impact of Analytics Outside Baseball

Does hiring a metrician pay off for basketball, football, and soccer teams? Have teams that have innovated in the use of statistical analysis to assist in personnel or strategy decisions benefitted? As with baseball, these are not easy questions to answer.

Suppose you are a metrician on an NBA team. You are assured that your statistical analysis will matter in team decision making because you are also the GM. Next, assume that you have examined the rosters of the last twenty-five teams that have won an NBA championship and you noticed that in twenty-four of those cases, the championship team had an all-time Top 50 player on the roster. You conclude that for your team to be a top competitor, it needs to hire at least one of the top ten players in the league. That's the easy part.

How do you get one of these players? If your team lacks the better prospects in the league, then it is not likely you'll be able to trade for a superstar.[29] Because of the salary cap and the Bird Exception, signing a superstar via free agency is an improbable option. The best option might be to shoot for the bottom of the standings and hope to get an early draft pick. Because of the NBA draft lottery, even this strategy (which some teams appear to follow) is uncertain.[30] There are, of course, permutations of these strategies, but the point should be clear: given the rigidity of the NBA's labor market, it is never a simple matter to put together a winning team—no matter how perceptive your statistical analysis might be.

That said, there is little evidence that those teams leading the way with analytics have fared better than the teams with more traditional approaches. To be sure, Grousbeck's Celtics benefitted from an elementary analytical insight, but not one that required complex statistical skills.

Similar to basketball and football, in soccer the nondiscrete and interdependent nature of play makes it substantially more difficult to identify compelling and practical performance metrics. One prominent soccermetrics blogger, Graham MacAree, commented:

> There seems to be a perception that football [meaning soccer in U.S. vernacular] statistics are entering some sort of golden age. With the proliferation of statistics sites such as WhoScored and EPL Index, not to mention the massive popularity of OPta's Twitter feeds and the Guardian's sadly-discontinued Chalkboard service, it's not hard to see why. Information is available where previously there was none.
>
> But anyone claiming that the *Moneyball* revolution is under way in football is sadly mistaken. The current statistics fail (and fail utterly) at passing Bill James' language test. If a player makes two fewer tackles than average but one more interception with more completed passes, for example, we have no way of figuring out how to put those statistics into context. What we currently have are numbers, not meaning.[31]

MacAree then continues on a more sanguine note: "Football is a complicated game . . . but . . . There's obviously some structure in the sport, and that alone is proof that we're not looking at an impossible problem."

Relatedly, a debate about the significance of statistical analysis erupted shortly after Lionel Messi broke an international record by scoring his eighty-sixth goal during the 2012 calendar year in the top division of the Spanish soccer league (La Liga). The former manager of Messi's Barcelona team, Pep Guardiola, declared that neither words nor statistics can adequately describe Messi's impact on a game. The only way to grasp Messi's impact, Guardiola declared, is to watch him play in the virtuosity of the moment.[32] Of course, the very fact that Messi broke a scoring record suggests that his talent can be described, at least in part, by numbers.

In the NFL, with the possible exception of the New England Patriots, there appears to be little correlation between the adoption of analytics and playing field success. Football metricians, however, do seem to have contributed important insights with regard to game strategy. The most significant, and one on which there is unanimity, is that coaches are too conservative on fourth down. Yet, according to a recent study by Football Outsiders, over the period 1992–2011 there has been no increased tendency for coaches to be more aggressive on fourth down.[33]

Football game strategy can also be informed regarding the best choices for approaching overtime, when to challenge a call, or when to rush three versus four linemen. Tabulating the experience of other teams against various opponents can help inform a team's tactics. Still, opening up these questions to statistical analysis also geometrically increases the potential processing of data and threatens to overwhelm GMs and coaches alike. In a world where the assimilation of such mountains of information and its analysis is new, the obstacles to its effective use are manifold. Thus, even though developing analytical insights in football with regard to game strategy may be more forthcoming than with personnel decisions, the cultural divide between the coaching staff and metricians in the front office is still wide and has held back what appears to be desirable change in game strategy.[34]

Ben Alamar and Vijay Mehrotra have aptly commented on the cultural chasm in NFL front offices: "Most decision-makers have little to no experience or training in the methods and tools of analytics, and as such are not well-equipped to evaluate the landscape of options. The result is that some organizations start small, at best thinking very incrementally about analytics and at worst simply adding a small amount of staff and/or software as window dressing. Meanwhile, other organizations have absolutely no idea of how to begin and thus simply do nothing."[35]

Of course, much of this observation also applies to baseball. Yet, outside baseball, analytics got a later start, tends to be more proprietary, and struggles with the less tractable nature of the sports themselves.

One football GM told a *New York Times* reporter: "Ideally, you want the objective and subjective to match up. The NFL is about resource allocation—you have a certain number of salary cap dollars and draft picks. If you found any area of the market that may be undervalued, you want to keep that information. At the end of the day, the tape is going to be our first choice. They have to look good on film."[36]

Analytics outside baseball, while growing, still seems to be taking its baby steps, mostly outside of public view.

6

Analytics and the Business of Baseball

Quantitative analysis has been increasingly introduced over the last two decades to understand the business of baseball (and other sports). It has been applied to a variety of issues, such as efficient ticket pricing, regulation of secondary ticket market policies, impact of stadiums and teams on a local economy, threshold city size for hosting a team, franchise valuation, the relationship between player development expenditures or major league payroll and team performance, labor market institutions, and optimal competitive balance, among others. Entire books have been written about these subjects, so in this brief chapter we only wish to illustrate an area of this research that directly affects the sabermetric concerns of player performance and team strategy.

It is the received wisdom that sports leagues, in order to command the interest and attention of an adequate fan base, must attain a certain degree of competitive balance across all the teams in a league. Without such a modicum of balance, the uncertainty that drives the suspense and excitement of league games and championship seasons is compromised, and game attendance as well as television ratings will suffer.[1]

Exactly how much balance is needed to maximize league revenues in the short and long runs, however, has never been established. Moreover, it is clear that the optimal degree of balance varies considerably between open and closed league systems, as well as from league to league within each system.

Competitive Balance in European Soccer Leagues

Notably, the soccer leagues in Europe, which operate with an open, promotion/relegation structure, demand less balance. This is because several contests during the league year are of interest to the fans: winning the league, not being relegated, gaining a berth in the following year's Champions League or Europa competition, along with various domestic competitions. In contrast, in the U.S. closed leagues, gaining a postseason berth and winning the championship is all that really matters.

Two other factors are also prominently at work. First, for a fan of Manchester United, Bayern Munich, Barcelona, InterMilan, or any other team, the two biggest prizes are winning the domestic league and winning the pan-European Champions League. If there is too much balance in the domestic league, then the domestic league's best teams will not have the requisite resources to dominate in the pan-European competition. Therefore, the European football leagues generally engage in much less revenue sharing than the U.S. leagues.

Second, the promotion/relegation leagues contain an automatic balancing mechanism that is not present in closed leagues. In open leagues the number of teams that play in a particular city is ultimately determined by market forces; thus, there have been between five and seven teams from greater London in the English Premier League in recent years. In the closed leagues, the market power of large city teams is protected by administrative controls exercised by the league monopoly. No team in the English Premier League contains the natural geographic advantage that, for instance, the New York Yankees or Los Angeles Dodgers have in Major League Baseball.

Competitive Balance in U.S. Sports Leagues

For these reasons, the U.S. closed leagues all depend on the equal distribution of 100 percent of central television, radio, Internet, licensing, and other revenue sources generated by the league office. They also all now have a supplementary revenue sharing system. In the NFL, which has had extensive revenue sharing since the league's inception in the early 1920s, the policy is the most penetrating, encompassing about 75 percent of all league-wide revenues. In the NHL, NBA, and MLB, where either little or no revenue sharing was present at the beginning of the leagues, the amount of shared revenue is less than 30 percent of league-wide revenues. Naturally, team owners from large cities in the latter leagues have a tendency to resist additional sharing because they paid a much higher price for their franchises than did the owners from small cities. They tend to view such sharing as confiscatory. The conflicts among owners over revenue sharing frequently spill out into labor conflicts and other inefficiencies.

Among those leagues that did not begin with revenue sharing, MLB has the most extensive sharing. MLB's supplementary system was introduced after the devastating 1994-1995 strike and has been expanded steadily, from under $30 million being shared in 1995 to nearly $400 million in 2012. Via various formulae, MLB has transferred these quantities of revenue from the high-revenue teams to the low-revenue teams. The basic idea has been twofold: on the one hand, by taking revenue away from the rich teams, to reduce high team payrolls, and, on the other, by giving revenue to the poor teams, to raise low team payrolls. That is, the system is supposed to result in payroll compression, which, in turn, is supposed to promote greater performance balance across the teams.[2]

Note that one issue here is that the explanatory power of payroll on win percentage in MLB, while usually statistically significant since 1990, tends to vary between 10 and 35 percent in any given year. This means that between 10 and 35 percent of the variation of a team's win percentage in a particular season is explained by that team's major league payroll. Or, stated differently, between 65 and 90 percent of the variation in win percentage in any year is explained by factors other than team payroll. This implies that even if MLB's system of revenue sharing resulted in appreciable payroll compression, the impact on the compression of win percentages may be less noticeable. Nonetheless, it is reasonable to assert that greater payroll compression will raise the probability of more compression (reduction in standard deviation) in team win percentages.

It is also interesting to note for our purposes that the use of inferior performance metrics (e.g., batting average instead of OBP or OPS) will tend

Table 6. Relationship Between Team Payroll and Team Win Percentage, 2003–2011

	2003	2004	2005	2006	2007	2008	2009	2010	2011
R^2	0.155	0.343	0.190	0.245	0.323	0.141	0.325	0.167	0.157
Three-Year Moving Average	0.249	0.229	0.259	0.253	0.236	0.263	0.211	0.217	

to lower the correlation between payroll and performance, while the use of improved metrics will tend to raise this correlation. That is, since improved metrics, by definition, show a tighter relationship with win percentage, their adoption will enable teams to allocate payroll more efficiently and increase the correlation between payroll and win percentage. If the spread of sabermetric knowledge within baseball has resulted in improved metrics over the last decade, then, other things equal, we should witness an increased correlation between payroll and win percentage. In Table 6, we show what has happened to the relationship between payroll and win percentage since the publication of *Moneyball* in 2003.

The first line in the table shows the R^2 or the percent of the variation in team win percentage that is explained by the variation in team payroll.[3] The second line is a three-year moving average of the same in order to smooth out the inevitable random year-to-year fluctuations. It is very difficult to identify a clear trend from the data on either line.[4] This, of course, doesn't mean that the new metrics are not valuable or that the spread of sabermetric knowledge is not happening. It simply means that these tests are abstracting from other pertinent information and are inconclusive.

The MLB Experience with Revenue Sharing and Competitive Balance

To properly grasp the empirical effect of revenue sharing on MLB's competitive balance, it is instructive to consider the trend before supplementary revenue sharing was introduced in 1996. Table 7 depicts the ratio of the standard deviation of win percentages to the idealized standard deviation of win percentages (RSD) since 1903. The lower the ratio, the greater the competitive balance. (The idealized standard deviation is that which would obtain if talent were equally distributed across all teams, given the number of games played in a season.[5] The RSD is the most commonly used measure of competitive balance, because it facilitates comparisons within a league over time or between leagues. It explicitly controls for the fact that the more games in a season's schedule, e.g., 154 versus 162 over time within baseball, or 16 versus 162 between the NFL and MLB, the less important chance will be in determining the distribution of team win percentages. Thus, we would expect leagues playing more games on the yearly schedule to have a lower standard deviation of win percentages.)

By the RSD ratio, there is a clear historical trend toward greater balance in MLB that runs through the 1980s. The ratio remains constant in the 1990s, halting the historical trend, the decade during which MLB's supplemental revenue sharing system was introduced. The ratio then proceeds to increase in the 2000s, reversing the historical trend, a decade when MLB's revenue sharing roughly tripled to some $400 million annually.

The principal reason for the secular downward trend through the 1980s (i.e., toward greater balance) is long-term talent compression. This has occurred as the percentage of the population (from the United States and other

Table 7. Ratio of Standard Deviation to Idealized Standard Deviation (RSD)

Period	Average of AL and NL
1903–1910	3.00
1910–1919	2.52
1920–1929	2.35
1930–1939	2.58
1940–1949	2.41
1950–1959	2.29
1960–1969	2.10
1970–1979	1.90
1980–1989	1.70
1990–1999	1.70
2000–2009	1.86

baseball countries) that plays in the major leagues has decreased over time, since the population has grown considerably faster than the number of teams.[6]

Baseball's supplemental revenue sharing was introduced in 1996 and then extended in the name of increasing competitive balance. The basic idea was that taking money away from rich teams like the Yankees (whose revenue sharing bill surpassed $100 million in 2010) and giving it to poor teams like the Marlins (whose receipts surpassed $40 million) would lower the top payrolls and raise the bottom payrolls. The resulting payroll compression would result in a more equal dispersion of team win percentages, engendering greater balance. Yet the RSD reported in Table 7 suggests that the outcome didn't match the expectations. What happened? Let us take a closer look.

Table 8 breaks down the changes in the RSD during different collective bargaining periods. Here it is seen more clearly that the increase in the ratio during the 1990s is coterminous with the introduction of the new supplemental revenue sharing system in the 1996-2002 CBA—a period during which the amount of revenue sharing grew from under $30 million to over $160 million. During the next CBA period, 2003-2006, the ratio creeps up, but not by a statistically significant margin. Then, during the 2007-2011 CBA, the ratio begins to modestly turn down, almost returning to its level in the early 1990s.

Since the correlation between team payroll and win percentage is far from perfect and since the presumed mechanism for promoting balance is via the narrowing of team payrolls, it makes sense to see how the increase in revenue sharing impacted the distribution of team payrolls. The coefficient of variation in team payrolls over the CBA periods is depicted in Table 9. (The coefficient of variation is the standard deviation divided by the mean; it allows for more meaningful intertemporal comparisons of distribution as the values in a data series grow.)

Table 8. Ratio of Standard Deviation to Idealized
Standard Deviation (RSD) During CBAs

Period	Average of AL and NL
1990–1995	1.67
1996–2002	1.89
2003–2006	1.90
2007–2011	1.72

Table 9. Payroll Coefficient of Variation

1985–1990	0.257
1991–1995	0.305
1996–2002	0.397
2003–2006	0.435
2007–2011	0.404

The evidence here is that the leveling of the RSD during 2003–2006 was not a function of payroll leveling, but that the subsequent RSD leveling during the 2007–2011 CBA may well have resulted from the narrowing of payroll differentials.

Before turning to our explanation of this pattern, it is important to consider other indices of competitive balance, such as balance between seasons. Table 10 looks at the degree of rotation among bottom dwellers in the American League (teams that finish last in their division) and Table 11 considers the same in the National League. Obviously, it would be in the interests of each league not to have the same teams finishing last each year. The more rotation at the bottom, the greater the perceived balance in the league. Table 10 shows that the percent of AL teams finishing last among all MLB teams fell steadily from 33 percent during the first half of the 1990s to 20 percent during the first half of the 2000s, but then increased modestly to 23 percent during the second half of the 2000s. Overall, this is not an encouraging record during this period of sharply increased revenue sharing, although it is consistent with the notion that the 2007–2011 CBA brought a change for the better. Table 11 shows that the percent of NL teams finishing last has declined steadily throughout these four quinquennia, from 40.7 percent during the early 1990s to 26.7 percent during the last period.

On the top end, considering whether teams from large markets are more likely to make the playoffs than teams from small markets, and how this has changed over time, the evidence in Table 12 is not encouraging either. Here the teams are put in quintiles, according to the population of their host city. Table 12 shows that the teams in the top 20 percent of markets substantially increased their average number of playoff appearances per year between the 1996–2002 CBA and the 2003–2006 CBA, while the bottom 20 percent sharply decreased the number of their playoff berths up to the CBA of 2007–2011. During the latter CBA, the number at the top stabilizes while the number at the bottom increases.

Table 10. Rotation on the Bottom, American League

Period	East	Central	West	Total Different	Percentage Different
1990–1994	Yankees	Twins		9	33.3%
	Indians	Angels			
	Red Sox	Mariners			
	Brewers	A's			
	Tigers	Brewers	Angels		
1995–1999	Blue Jays	Twins	A's	8	27.6%
	Tigers	Royals	Angels		
	Blue Jays	Royals	A's		
	Rays	Tigers	A's		
	Rays	Twins	Angels		
2000–2004	Rays	Twins	Rangers	6	20.0%
	Rays	Royals	Rangers		
	Rays	Tigers	Rangers		
	Rays	Tigers	Rangers		
	Blue Jays	Royals	Mariners		
2005–2009	Rays	Royals	Mariners	7	23.3%
	Rays	Royals	Mariners		
	Rays	Royals	Rangers		
	Orioles	Tigers	Mariners		
	Orioles	Royals	A's		

Thus, by all measures considered here, competitive balance in MLB appears to have deteriorated as the quantity of revenue sharing from rich to poor teams grew since the system was first introduced in 1996 through 2006. We are now ready to ask why this has occurred and why this trend may have begun to change with the 2007–2011 CBA.

Table 11. Rotation on the Bottom, National League

Period	East	Central	West	Total Different	Percentage Different
1990–1994	Cards	Braves		11	40.7%
	Expos	Astros			
	Phillies	Dodgers			
	Mets	Padres			
	Marlins	Cubs	Padres		
1995–1999	Expos	Pirates	Giants	9	31.0%
	Phillies	Pirates	Giants		
	Phillies	Cubs	Padres		
	Marlins	Pirates	Diamondbacks		
	Marlins	Cubs	Rockies		
2000–2004	Phillies	Cubs	Padres	9	30.0%
	Expos	Pirates	Rockies		
	Mets	Brewers	Padres		
	Mets	Brewers	Padres		
	Expos	Brewers	Diamondbacks		
2005–2009	Nats	Pirates	Rockies	8	26.7%
	Nats	Cubs	Rockies		
	Marlins	Pirates	Giants		
	Nats	Pirates	Padres		
	Nats	Pirates	Diamondbacks		

Table 12. Average Playoff Berths per Year by Population Quintile

	CBA 1996–2002	CBA 2003–2006	CBA 2007–2011
Top	1.86	2.75	2.40
Second	2.14	1.50	1.60
Third	1.57	1.25	1.40
Fourth	1.29	2.00	1.80
Bottom	1.14	0.50	0.80

Changing Incentives and Improved Competitive Balance

As the size of the transfer in MLB's revenue sharing has grown rapidly at almost 20 percent per year since its introduction in 1996, the method for calculating each team's net payments and receipts has changed both during and between CBAs. The computation through 2006 depended on two basic systems: a straight pool plan and a split pool plan. The former taxes each team's net defined local revenue at the same rate and then redistributes it in equal shares to all teams.[7] The marginal tax rate in the straight pool system, thus, is equal for all teams. The split pool system taxes only the top teams and redistributes only to the bottom teams, in each case on the basis of how far the team's revenue deviates from the average team revenue. As a consequence of combining these two methods, the marginal tax rates between 1996 and 2006 were actually higher for the low revenue teams than for the high revenue teams. For instance, between 2003 and 2006, the marginal tax rate paid by the teams with above average revenue was approximately 39 percent, while that paid by teams with below average revenue was close to 48 percent.[8] The below average revenue teams "paid" a tax in the sense that when their revenue increased by $1, they received 48 cents less in transfers.

To illustrate, suppose the Dodgers and the Pirates were both considering the signing of a free agent pitcher and further suppose that each team estimated that the player would produce $10 million of additional revenue for the team. Given the differential marginal tax rates in the revenue sharing system that each team would face, the net (after sharing) incremental revenue for the Dodgers would be an estimated $6.1 million, while that for the Pirates would be $5.2 million. Thus, the bottom half of teams had a stronger disincentive to invest in improving team performance (such as by increasing payroll) than the top half.

This disincentive is compounded by the fact that teams experience different revenue elasticities with respect to increases in their win percentage. That is, depending on the size of the local market and the team's win percentage, the impact of an additional win on team revenue will vary, and often vary significantly, among teams.[9] For instance, an extra win will bring more revenue to a team in New York than a team in Kansas City. New York has more people with more income and more large corporations (to buy advertising, contract sponsorships, or purchase premium seating) than Kansas City, so the response to having a competitive team will be greater in New York than in Kansas City, other things being equal.

The other major factor that results in different revenue responses to wins (elasticities) across teams is a team's position in its league standings. A team that sits in last place with a .400 win percentage is unlikely to excite its fan base by winning an extra game and raising its win percentage to .406. But a team with a win percentage of .512 and is one game away from making the playoffs may experience a significant fan response from an extra win. Thus, we would expect teams with low win percentages to have low elasticities and teams with high win percentages to have high elasticities—though this may level off or even become negative at very high win percentage levels. The relationship between revenue and win percentage is depicted by a win curve.

Estimating a win curve for MLB with data from 1992 through 2009, using

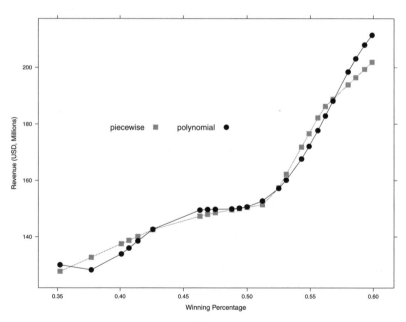

Figure 11. Win Curves: Estimated Average Relationship Between WPCT and Team Revenue

both a ninth degree polynomial and a piecewise (based on win percentage quintiles) regression with fixed team and year effects,[10] shows that the revenue is mildly
responsive to improved team performance up to a win percentage of around .500.
Between .500 and .570, the revenue response becomes very elastic; while above
.570 the response begins to level off. This relationship is depicted in Figure 11.

If low revenue teams face both a flatter win curve and a higher marginal
tax rate, it is unlikely in the extreme that transferring revenue to them will
lead to payroll compression. This pattern is only reinforced when low win
percentage teams are also the teams in the smaller markets. Thus, it should
not be surprising that MLB team payrolls did not experience compression
between 1996 and 2006.[11]

It is noteworthy, however, that MLB's 2007-2011 CBA rectified the regressive
tax rate. The primary distribution mechanism continued to be the straight pool
system, which accounted for approximately 65 percent of the total transfer. The
remaining transfer was based on team revenues in 2004-2005 and projected
revenues for 2006-2007.[12] Hence, the secondary distribution was based on fixed
revenues and was not affected by team actual revenue performance during the
2007-2011 period. The result is that each team faced close to identical marginal
tax rates of around 30 percent, and the disincentive for bottom teams to lift
payrolls that was built into earlier CBAs was eliminated during 2007-2011. This
observation helps to explain why the distribution of payrolls became modestly
more compressed since 2006 as well as why the RSD decreased.

The current 2012-2016 CBA solidifies the incentive gains achieved in the
previous CBA and introduces some new mechanisms that should further
promote balance. Among the new mechanisms, the Rule 4 amateur draft will
now be subject to a tax and cap plan, international signings will also be subject to a cap, and there will be a competitive balance lottery giving extra draft
picks to low finishing teams. The cap and tax plan works like this. The team
with the lowest win percentage the prior year is allocated the highest cap,
while the team with the highest win percentage is given the lowest cap.[13] For
2012, the per team caps run from $4.47 million to $11.49 million. If a team exceeds its limit, it will be subjected to a tax of between 75 and 100 percent and
face the possible loss of future picks. These changes are all explicitly designed
to give the low revenue teams more picks and to maximize the possibility

that they will be able to sign the picks they make. Baseball, of course, has also added a second wild card team in each league, commencing in 2012, which will make for more exciting pennant races and provide for more opportunities for postseason appearances.

The foregoing discussion has omitted several elements that are part of the context of MLB's economic system and, instead, has focused on the role of incentives in the design of an effective system to promote competitive balance. Economic theory teaches that incentives matter and MLB has provided a laboratory over the past fifteen years that corroborates this concept. Of course, designing a system and implementing it are two different matters; the latter always confronts the reality of political divisions and constraints. In this regard, MLB is no different than any other sports league or decision-making body.

7

Estimating the Impact of Sabermetrics

Sabermetricians measure performance—mostly performance on the field, but also in the dugout and in the front office. They seek to inform us through new metrics and analysis what produces wins and profits.

In this chapter, we turn the tables by endeavoring to measure the output of sabermetricians. In Chapter 1, we expressed skepticism about the story told by Michael Lewis in *Moneyball*, or at least about the details of that story. Lewis may have missed a few basic points and misrepresented several others, but that doesn't mean that the underlying message was wrong. If *Moneyball* was nothing more than an intriguing fable, it is unlikely that sabermetrics would have spread like wildfire throughout team front offices, as it did in the ensuing years, and as we documented in Chapter 2.

Certain sabermetric insights, whether they originated in the work of F. C. Lane, Allan Roth, George Lindsay, Earnshaw Cook, Pete Palmer, Bill James, Vörös McCracken, Tom Tippett, or others, are of indisputable value. There is, for instance, no rational reason to think that batting average is a greater contributor to wins than on-base percentage, that fielding percentage is more important than DER, or that ERA is a more meaningful indicator of future pitching prowess than FIP.

Indeed, consider the following statistical evidence. One way to parse the relative importance of the saber-inspired metrics of OBP, DER, and FIP versus the traditional metrics of BA, FPCT, and ERA is to run a regression of win percentage on each set of three variables. We did this for the years 1985 through 2011 and the results were clear. For model (1) below, the coefficient of determination, or R², is 0.80. That is, 80 percent of the variance of win percentage is explained by the variance of OBP, DER and FIP. Conversely, the R^2 for model (2) is 0.69.

$$(1) \text{ WPCT} = f(\text{OBP, DER, FIP})$$
$$(2) \text{ WPCT} = f(\text{BA, FPCT, ERA})$$

Thus, the saber-inspired metrics explain 11 percent more of the variance in win percentage than do the conventional metrics. Other things being equal, this suggests that a GM making use of saber-inspired metrics will have an advantage of 11 percentage points toward putting together a winning team, as opposed to a non-saber-inspired GM.

But this is easier said than done, as there are many obstacles to move from saber-inspired metrics to building a better team. First, sabermetrics itself is a moving target, since the theory and practice have evolved considerably over the past twenty years. On many issues, there is no consensus as to what the correct sabermetric interpretation even is. For example, the debate about the value of stolen bases continues to this day. Most people who have studied the issue have found that the cost of the out lost by getting caught stealing is roughly two times as large as the value gained by swiping a base. This insight led many teams, most notably the A's and Red Sox, who were purported adherents of sabermetrics, to become extremely conservative on the basepaths. In fact, among the last twenty team-seasons with the fewest stolen bases, half belong to the A's and Red Sox, with no other franchise appearing more than once on the list.

However, suppose that you were Tampa Bay, and that you already had Carl Crawford on your team. You knew that Crawford stole bases with a historically high success rate (approaching 90 percent), and so you were convinced that by any reasonable accounting, his baserunning would make a positive contribution to your offense. Should you discourage him from stealing bases? Of course not. Thus, while the prevalence of stolen bases is not a perfect metric for estimating sabermetric intensity, it does produce several notable true positives in this context.

Second, sometimes the metric in question is easy to identify at the team level, but difficult to identify at the player level. For instance, DER, or defensive efficiency rating,[1] is roughly equal to 1 – BABIP, where BABIP is batting average for balls is play. Hence, DER measures the ability of the team in the field to convert a ball put in play (i.e., not a home run, not a walk, and not a strike out) into an out. This measure is broader than the conventional fielding percentage, because the latter just measures whether fielders can convert a ball hit in their range (whatever it may be) into an out, whereas DER also encompasses the fielders' ability to get to the ball (their positioning, jump, speed, balance, etc.) and, if necessary, throw it in a timely and accurate manner to the relevant base. One issue is that DER is not a pure measure of fielding prowess because part of it measures luck (whether balls happen to be hit right at a player or take a bad hop), part of it measures whether the fielders were positioned properly by the coaches, part of it measures whether the pitcher threw the pitch to the part of the plate that was signaled, and part measures the opposing team's hitting (how hard and at what trajectory a ball was hit).

While measuring DER for a team is straightforward, it cannot be observed directly for an individual player. In order to capture an individual fielder's defensive prowess, we have to know his sure-handedness, the accuracy and strength of his arm, his instinct for positioning, the jump he gets on a hit ball, the speed and balance with which he runs to the ball, the velocity, trajectory, and spin of the hit ball, and so on. While there have been forays into quantifying these factors for individual players, such as UZR (as we discussed in Chapter 4), these measures are still in the early stages of development, display erratic results, and are often proprietary (meaning that the details of the computation are unknown to the general public, making it difficult, if not impossible, to assess the validity of the underlying methodology). Thus, while the use of DER gives us good predictive powers at the team level, a GM would have a formidable task in discerning how to select individual players based on this concept.

Nonetheless, although the precise quantification of an individual player's fielding skill may be elusive statistically, the recognition of the importance of DER in team success is significant in itself. Even without a new, reliable metric, teams can train scouts and analysts to more closely track a player's defensive skill set, either through live or video observation, and, thereby, improve its capacity to build a defensively strong team. As we will discover, it appears that the Tampa Bay Rays have done precisely this and that the team's remarkable success since 2008 owes much to this development.

Third, another link between identifying more useful metrics and engendering strong team performance resides in a team's development system and its coaches. Players' skill sets and proclivities are not static; they change and develop over time. A GM might make what appears to be an optimal player acquisition, but unless that player is put in the right environment and developed appropriately, the payoff for the team might be small.

Fourth, the next conundrum for the saber-savvy GM is that other teams may have identified the same new metrics, raising the market demand for the associated abilities and, hence, the price for the new player skills. If the new metric is 10 percent more closely associated with wins, but the price of the related skill rises 10 percent, then the saber-savvy GM may be no better off. We will consider this potential dynamic in more detail shortly.

Fifth, suppose our insightful GM does everything right and identifies an ideal draft pick, free agent, or player to be acquired in a trade. The draft pick might go to another team with an earlier pick, the free agent might want to play in a different city or accept a higher offer, and the prospective trade might not be consummated for any number of reasons. Nothing is gained.

Sixth, a GM may receive good advice from a metrician, but choose to ignore it.

Last, an acquired player may become injured or feel less comfortable with the players and coaches on the new team, and, thus, be less productive than anticipated. Baseball is a game infused with chance and uncertainty . . . and may it stay that way.

For any one of the above reasons, the nexus between a sabermetric insight and greater team success can be disrupted. Accordingly, measuring the output (or value) of sabermetricians is not an easy matter. Nevertheless, since sabermetricians purport to measure the contribution of others, it makes sense, despite the inherent complications, to attempt to measure the contribution of sabermetricians.

Hence, after some ten years of experience with self-conscious sabermetrics in baseball's front offices, we ask: What's the record? Has the adoption of sabermetrics paid off for teams? To answer the questions, we basically follow a two-step analysis. First, we attempt to identify the intensity of sabermetric practice (saber-intensity) across baseball's thirty teams. Second, we see how this intensity is correlated with team performance, after controlling for team payroll.

Saber-Intensity in Theory

Identifying saber-intensity might sound more straightforward than it is. If we try to measure saber-intensity by counting front office personnel doing sabermetric analysis, we encounter various obstacles. The first is that team organizational charts (or even media guides) are not always easy to obtain, not always complete and not always clear. As indicated in Chapter 2, people doing sabermetric analysis don't always have "sabermetric" titles. The second is that in many instances the role of scout and the role of sabermetrician are less and less distinct—increasingly the scout uses new statistical metrics and the sabermetrician employs video to analyze player performance. The third is that what happens in a baseball operations statistical office does not always connect with what happens in the GM's office or what happens on the field.

Another confounding factor is that sometimes decisions have all the earmarks of being sabermetrically inspired, but are in reality the result of nothing more than gut instinct, idiosyncrasy, or luck. Take, for instance, the signing of free agent David Ortiz by the Red Sox in 2003. The new ownership at the time already had a strong reputation for being sabermetrically oriented. Principal owner John Henry had attempted to lure Billy Beane away from the Oakland A's, had signed Bill James to be the lead statistical analyst for the Red Sox, and had hired the 28-year-old, statistically oriented Yale graduate Theo Epstein to be the team's GM. Henry's own background in finance involved developing statistical models to track commodities and currency prices.

By 2004, the new Red Sox ownership had assembled enough talent to win the team's first World Series since 1918. The conventional wisdom is that the Red Sox success was another feather in the cap of sabermetrics. Ortiz's last three years with the Minnesota Twins showed a mediocre batting average of .265, but he demonstrated both power (isolated power of .205) and plate discipline (he walked in nearly 11 percent of his plate appearances).[2] He was a sabermetric diamond in the rough.

Pre-eminent baseball writer and television commentator Tom Verducci told Andrew Zimbalist that the Red Sox were a clear illustration of the success of sabermetrics and that the signings of Bill Mueller and David Ortiz were prime examples of the method at work. Verducci is not alone in this assessment, and there is little question that sabermetrics had a hand in the assembling of the Red Sox 2004 roster (though a good deal of credit has to go to the team's GM from 1994 through March 2002, Dan Duquette).[3]

But what about David Ortiz—the team's offensive leader in 2004, with an OBP of .380 and an OPS of .983, along with his forty-one homers and clutch hitting? It turns out that the signing of Ortiz had nothing to do with sabermetrics. Red Sox standout pitcher, Pedro Martinez knew Ortiz from playing with him in the Dominican Republic winter leagues and urged the front office to sign him, despite Ortiz's history of knee problems. (Of course, the front office exercised the judgment to act on Martinez's recommendation.) The rest is history.

Or, consider the case of Dustin Pedroia. Pedroia was the sixty-fifth pick in the 2004 amateur draft. His physical attributes were unimpressive, but a careful analysis of his numbers commended him to some. Traditional scouting based on the five tools would have had him fall well below the second round of the draft.[4] While the Red Sox sabermetrician-in-chief Bill James liked Pedroia, he did not recommend that the Red Sox spend a second-round pick on him. That decision was made higher up. Pedroia, of course, went on to become one of the best second basemen and premier overall players in baseball over the past decade, winning the American League's MVP Award in 2008. Many would have credited sabermetric insight for Boston's prescient selection of Pedroia in the second round of the draft. But Nate Silver says what distinguished Pedroia is something that only intelligent scouts could have seen—his exemplary attitude and mental attributes.[5]

Thus, attempting to judge saber-intensity from outside an organization and based on an organizational chart or media guide is problematic. We choose instead to develop objective indicators of a team's approach to roster-building and game strategy.

As discussed in earlier chapters, one of the most fundamental of the sabermetric insights, and one emphasized in *Moneyball*, is that walks are almost as good as singles; or, more precisely, both walks and singles share the essential and important characteristic that they do not use up one of the three outs per inning and they each result in a man reaching first base.[6] For this reason, along with the fact (detailed in Chapter 3) that OBP is more closely associated with runs scored, sabermetricians have long argued that OBP (on-base percentage) is a superior metric to BA (batting average).

OBP, then, is a useful measure of how sabermetrically inspired a team's roster is in practice. Higher OBPs can result both from the signing of players from outside the organization and from coaches emphasizing the importance of being selective at the plate (although not all hitters can assimilate this skill). It is not sufficient, however, to simply compare one team's OBP to another's to identify each team's saber-intensity. This is because teams with a higher payroll are likely to have players with higher BAs as well as higher OBPs. Instead, to neutralize the effect of payroll, we consider the ratio of OBP to BA for each team. We call this metric *onbase*.

Since ballparks have different dimensions with regard to the distance of the fences from home plate, the amount of foul territory, prevailing wind patterns, effect of the batter's eye in centerfield, and so on, teams that play half their games in certain parks will either be advantaged or disadvantaged with regard to certain metrics. For both OBP and BA, as well as for other performance metrics used in this chapter, we adjust for park and other factors; our adjustment methodology is described in the Appendix.

It will likely come as little surprise that Oakland dominates the list of teams that score highly in the *onbase* metric, claiming seven of the top twenty-five spots, as shown in Table 13. (The values are normalized; the average score for an MLB team is 1.00, so the 1999 Oakland A's, with the highest score during 1985–2011, were 7.2 percent above the overall average.) It is also noteworthy that the *Moneyball* year of 2002, as designated by Michael Lewis, does not make it onto this list, although the teams from Oakland's three previous seasons do.[7]

Table 13. Highest *onbase* Scores

Year	Team	onbase	Year	Team	onbase
1999	Oakland	1.072	1991	Oakland	1.049
1991	Detroit	1.067	2004	New York Yankees	1.049
2010	Tampa Bay	1.065	1997	Florida	1.049
1985	Los Angeles Angels	1.061	1989	Detroit	1.048
1990	Baltimore	1.060	2011	Tampa Bay	1.048
2006	Boston	1.059	1994	Detroit	1.048
2006	Oakland	1.055	2001	Oakland	1.047
1992	New York Mets	1.054	2007	Oakland	1.047
1992	Oakland	1.053	2000	Oakland	1.047
2003	New York Yankees	1.053	1987	Atlanta	1.046
2011	New York Yankees	1.053	2010	New York Yankees	1.046
2000	Seattle	1.052	1998	St. Louis	1.044
1986	Los Angeles Angels	1.050			

Although OBP is probably the best-known indicator of saber-intensity, there are several other candidates. In the area of game strategy, sabermetricians have long observed that, under more circumstances than many people think, it does not make sense to sacrifice bunt, and thereby give up one of the three outs in an inning (see discussion in Chapter 3). Both the expected run matrix and linear weights methods show that on average using the sacrifice bunt does not increase run output.[8] Because of the fact that pitchers bat in the National League and not the American League, the NL has a higher rate of using the sacrifice bunt. Hence, as with our other metrics, our sacrifice bunt metric is calibrated relative to the average number of sacrifice bunts in the league. We call this metric *sacbunt*.[9]

Similarly, sabermetricians have maintained that unless a baserunner can steal bases with a high success rate (generally over 65 percent), the extra base gained is not worth the potential loss of an out. Accordingly, other things equal, high saber-intensity teams will tend to use the sacrifice bunt and stolen base strategies more judiciously. Naturally, some teams find themselves with superlative baserunners on their rosters who may be successful in 90 percent or more of their stolen base attempts. There would be no reason to restrain the aggressive instincts of such stolen base leaders. Accordingly, our metric for saber-intensive base theft strategy is based on the difference 0.18 SB - 0.32 CS, where SB is stolen base and CS is caught stealing, which equals the expected run value gained from a successful stolen base minus the expected run value lost from an unsuccessful attempt. Our stolen base metric is *brun*.

Another area of sabermetric focus, although the initial insight dates back to Henry Chadwick in 1872, has been fielding. The traditional measure of fielding proficiency is fielding percentage (FPCT). As indicated above, this metric does not take account of a fielder's ability to get to a ball, nor in many instances to make a strong, accurate throw. A standard sabermetric measure is DER, or defensive efficiency rating. DER encompasses a team's fielders' ability to reach balls in play and to make the necessary throws. Our metric here is the ratio of DER to FPCT, or *der*.[10]

As discussed in Chapter 4, initiated by the work of Vörös McCracken during 1999–2001, sabermetricians have argued that the traditional measure of pitching performance, earned run average or ERA, is significantly limited. ERA is dependent on team fielding and good fortune. McCracken observed that the typical pitcher's BABIP (batting average on balls in play) showed only a very low correlation from one year to the next. In contrast, the typical pitcher's home runs allowed, strikeouts, and walks showed high consistency over time. Accordingly, sabermetricians developed a new metric, called Fielding Independent Pitching (FIP), as a truer measure of pitching skill and performance. Because FIP is constructed according to a formula that typically compresses its values between 3 and 4, it is not possible to derive a mathematically meaningful measure from the ratio of FIP to ERA.[11] In this case, since the saber-savvy metric FIP is lower for better pitchers, we take its inverse, 1/FIP, to arrive at our pitching index *fip*.

Our final metric of saber-intensity represents the ability to hit for power. The standard sabermetric measure of a batter's power is Isolated Power (ISO). In contrast, the conventional measure of power that incorporates all extra base hits is slugging percentage (SLG). As is well known, SLG gives one point for a single, two for a double, three for a triple, and four for a home run and divides the total points by the number of at bats. This relative weighting of base hits does not accord with their relative contribution to runs produced; moreover, it includes singles which do not represent power hitting and it weights triples as representing 50 percent more power than doubles, even though the evidence suggests that triples are not necessarily hit harder or further than doubles. ISO, in contrast, usually scores doubles and triples equally and does not include singles.[12] By the same logic as used for earlier metrics, our measure of saber-intensity with regard to power is ISO divided by SLG, represented by *iso*.

On the basis of these six metrics (*onbase, sacbunt, brun, der, fip, iso*), we construct a composite index of saber-intensity for each team. Before we present our findings, however, it is necessary to take a short detour on shifting labor inefficiencies to provide a context for their interpretation.

Identifying Labor Market Inefficiencies

One of the central tenets of the moneyball philosophy lies in the relationship between the value of certain skills (such as having a good eye, as manifested in the walk rate) in producing wins and the value of these skills in baseball's labor market. If there is a disjuncture between these values, then there is a market inefficiency that the astute general manager can exploit.

On one level, it is surprising that baseball's labor market would have such inefficiencies. After all, we are better able to measure an individual's productivity in baseball than in practically any other industry. There are measurements in baseball for just about everything. Yet there is a good deal of evidence that such inefficiencies have existed.

What is true, however, is that the abundance of publicly available data on player productivity, team payrolls and team success makes it unlikely that the inefficiencies will persist. Other teams will soon notice the imbalance between value and price, and change their behavior. Thus, the A's apparently discovered the inefficiency that walks were undervalued in the late 1990s. The evidence we present below is that the undervaluation of walks began to adjust prior to 2003.

As we consider the evidence, it is important to keep in mind that baseball's labor market has built-in rigidities. First, during the first three years of major league experience,[13] players are under reserve to their teams. That is, players are not free to go into the labor market to receive salary bids that reflect their performance; rather, they belong to the team and usually receive MLB's minimum salary ($490,000 in 2013) or a salary close to it. Until the player has six full years of major league experience, the player cannot go to the labor market as a free agent, but he is eligible for salary arbitration. In the arbitration process, the player's salary is expected to approach a free-market level. Many teams sign arbitration-eligible players to long-term contracts. After six years of major league experience, players become free agents and the better ones sign long-term contracts, many lasting for four, five, six, or more years.

Because of the fact that players under reserve have salaries divorced from their productivity and a large share of the other players have salaries that are based on their productivity from earlier years, it is not to be expected that salaries will adjust immediately once a market inefficiency is discovered. Thus, we would not expect, even if the publication of *Moneyball* were the catalyst to change the behavior of baseball front offices, that there would be a sudden, dramatic change in labor market skill valuations in 2004. Rather, the adjustment would come gradually, beginning in 2004. Yet, as we discussed in Chapter 1, change was already under way in baseball front offices prior to the publication of *Moneyball* and our evidence suggests that the labor market had already begun to shift prior to 2004. When we consider the return in salary to a player's walk rate (share of plate appearances when a player reaches base with a walk or hit by pitch), we find that the uptick begins in 2002 (Figure 12). Recall that if *Moneyball* were the catalyst for this correction, we would not even begin to see the correction before 2004. Also, as shown in Figure 12, the correction did accelerate in 2004, but then it seemed to reverse in the next two years.

We must be cautious, however, in placing too much emphasis on the year-to-year changes because there are random fluctuations in the annual labor market conditions (for instance, the number and quality of free agents available in any given year can vary considerably) that could impact these results. The final picture that emerges is the one described earlier: a market correction begins prior to the publication of *Moneyball*, accelerates after the publication probably to the point of overcorrection, and then adjusts moderately.

Nevertheless, if *Moneyball* did not initiate the labor market correction, it certainly contributed to it. Indeed, the return to the skill of working a walk

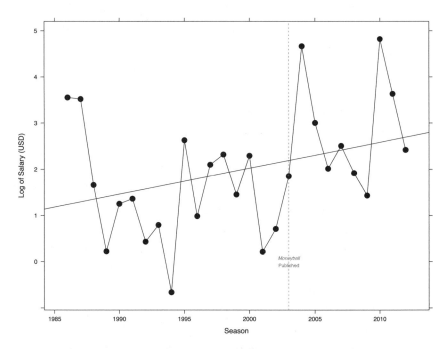

Figure 12. Estimated Labor Market Valuations, 1986–2012
Each dot represents the estimated increase in ln(Salary) for each additional unit of Eye
in the previous season. A trend line for Eye is indicated. Eye is walks plus hit by pitch
per plate appearance. See Appendix for fuller discussion.

increased by around 64 percent between the 1998–2002 and 2003–2007 periods.[14] Our evidence also indicates that the market may have overcorrected
slightly, as the return to the skill of walking fell by approximately 12 percent
during 2008–2012. As we shall see, the A's strategy shifted, suggesting that
Billy Beane perceived that he could no longer take advantage of the undervaluation of the skill of walking.[15]

Another way to consider the shifting labor market inefficiency is to evaluate the relative return to the walk rate versus the return to batting average. In
Table 14 we present the results of a regression of the log of Runs Scored (RS) on
the logs of Walk Rate (WR), Batting Average (BA), and Power.[16] The resulting
coefficients yield estimates of the elasticity of each batting skill on runs scored;

that is, the percent change in RS divided by the percent change in WR (or other hitting skill). For instance, the 0.267 coefficient indicates that during 1985–1997 a 1 percent increase in a team's walk rate increased the number of runs the team will score by 0.267 percent.[17] In Table 15, we present the results of a regression of the log of individual player salary on the logs of lagged WR, BA and Power. The 0.138 coefficient, for instance, indicates that during 1985–97 a 1 percent increase in a player's walk rate increased his (next year's) salary by 0.138 percent. For our purposes, it is interesting to follow row 1 in Table 15 across the different time periods. It shows that the salary return to a 1 percent increase in a player's walk rate increased in each of the next two time periods, 1998–2002 and 2003–2007, by 6 percent (from 0.138 to 0.146) and 64 percent (from 0.146 to 0.239), respectively, before turning down in 2008–2012. These results, of course, are consistent with the argument that teams began to assign greater value to a good eye and patience at the plate in the late 1990s and first years of the 2000s and that this growing return accelerated after the publication of *Moneyball*.

Table 14. Impact (Elasticity) of Walk Rate (WR), Batting Average (BA), and Power on Runs Scored (RS)

	1985–1997	*1998–2002*	*2003–2007*	*2008–2012*
WR	0.267	0.305	0.230	0.255
BA	1.671	1.850	1.960	1.690
Power	0.982	0.774	0.957	1.027

Table 15. Impact (Elasticity) of Walk Rate (WR), Batting Average (BA), and Power on Player Salary

	1985–1997	*1998–2002*	*2003–2007*	*2008–2012*
WR	0.138	0.146	0.239	0.211
BA	0.826	1.009	1.121	0.894
Power	0.920	1.178	1.213	0.978

It is also relevant to look at the returns to batter skills in relation to the productivity (runs produced) by each skill; that is, the ratio of the elasticity of salary to the elasticity of RS for each skill, as depicted in Table 16. Here we see that a similar pattern holds up over the periods. The salary return to WR relative to the run scoring contribution of WR accelerates during 2003–2007, and then falls off during 2008–2012. This pattern is consistent with our earlier contention that what might have been sound sabermetric advice about labor market strategy (exploiting the undervaluation of walks) ten years ago might not be sound advice in recent years. This insight must be kept in mind when evaluating the saber-intensity of team front offices.

Quantifying Saber-Intensity

The particular relevance of this pattern to our discussion is that, after the market correction, we should not expect saber-oriented teams to continue to emphasize player attributes that were previously undervalued. To wit, we would not expect the Oakland A's necessarily to continue to be among the top teams in walk rate or the ratio of OBP/BA (*onbase*). And, indeed, during the period 1998–2008, the A's led the major leagues in *onbase* with an index of 1.041, but then abruptly fell to an average of 1.005 during 2009–2011. Similarly, the A's strategy with regard to baserunning shifted abruptly as their index of runs created from a stolen base jumped by 60 percent from the 1998–2008 period to 2009–2011.

As presented above, however, we have developed six indicators of saber-intensity, and it is useful to consider their overall effect. To do this, we introduce a composite index of saber-intensity. In particular, we combine the six indicators by weighting them according to the contribution that each element of skill or strategy makes to a team's win percentage. To estimate this

Table 16. Relative Return to Batting Skills (lnSal/lnRS)

	1985–1997	1998–2002	2003–2007	2008–2012
WR	0.514	0.479	1.040	0.827
BA	0.495	0.545	0.572	0.530
Power	0.937	1.522	1.267	0.952

contribution we run a multiple regression of the log of win percentage on the logs of OBP, ISO, DER, FIP, baserunning (BRUN), and sacrifice bunts (SACBUNT). The resulting coefficients tell us the percentage contribution that each skill or strategy element makes to a team's win percentage. All the coefficients are statistically significant at standard levels,[18] and we weight the individual metrics according to these coefficients in our composite index, as follows.[19]

Saber-Intensity Weights: .237 OBP, .037 ISO, .290 FIP,

.433 DER, .001 BRUN, .002 SACBUNT

Note that DER has the highest weight, followed by FIP in a distant second, and then OBP close behind. Although ISO, BRUN and SACBUNT are all statistically significant at the .10 level or better, the magnitude of their impacts is much smaller. We then apply these weights to our six saber-intensity skill elements to generate our composite SI index. It is also of interest that the defensive and pitching components to the A's success in the early 2000s were virtually omitted from Lewis's analysis in *Moneyball*. This provides further corroboration of our contention that more of the A's success was attributable to their superior pitching staff than to their penchant for walking.

In Table 17 we present the top thirty scores in our saber-intensity index since 1985. Most of the names are familiar. The Atlanta Braves of the 1990s captured first place as well as four of the top eleven places in our composite index. While these teams were not known for embracing the sabermetric philosophy, the intelligence of their front office personnel was impressive and these teams were characterized by extremely strong pitching (with three Cy Young Award winners on the same team in Greg Maddux, Tom Glavine, and John Smoltz) and defense (with Otis Nixon, Rafael Belliard, Andruw Jones, Terry Pendleton, Ron Gant, and Marquis Grissom).[20] The 2007 Red Sox and the 2001 A's, two successful teams widely recognized for their saber-intensity, are in a near dead heat with the 1995 Braves. The championship 2004 Red Sox, the Oakland A's in 2003 and in 1990 are in fifth, seventh, and eighth place respectively. The 1990 A's were, of course, led by Sandy Alderson, with sabermetrician Eric Walker by his side, and featured players like Rickey Henderson (high walk rate) and

Dennis Eckersley (high strikeout-to-walk ratio) who would later be identified as sabermetric darlings. Beyond eighth place, there are few surprises with most of the teams inclined toward sabermetrics or with dominant pitching and tight defense (e.g., the 2008 Tampa Bay Rays). Our composite metric appears to correlate well with the prevailing wisdom on sabermetrically oriented clubs.

It is also instructive to consider how the teams rank over different time periods. For instance, during the 1992–97 period Atlanta received the highest

Table 17. Top Thirty Scores in Saber-Intensity (SI) Index, 1985–2011

	Year	Team	SI
1	1995	Atlanta	1.036
2	2007	Boston	1.036
3	2001	Oakland	1.035
4	1993	Atlanta	1.032
5	2004	Boston	1.032
6	1997	Atlanta	1.031
7	2003	Oakland	1.031
8	1990	Oakland	1.030
9	2011	Philadelphia	1.030
10	1995	Baltimore	1.029
11	1994	Atlanta	1.029
12	2008	Tampa Bay	1.028
13	2002	Arizona	1.028
14	1986	Los Angeles Angels	1.028
15	2008	Arizona	1.027
16	2003	New York Yankees	1.027
17	2009	Colorado	1.027
18	1999	Boston	1.026
19	2002	Oakland	1.026
20	1998	Atlanta	1.026
21	2000	Boston	1.026
22	2002	New York Yankees	1.026
23	1999	Atlanta	1.025
24	1998	New York Yankees	1.025
25	1999	New York Yankees	1.025
26	1996	Atlanta	1.024
27	2011	Tampa Bay	1.024
28	1991	Toronto	1.024
29	2010	Tampa Bay	1.024
30	2008	Chicago Cubs	1.024

average score, followed by Baltimore and Montreal, as shown in Table 18. During the immediate pre-*Moneyball* period, 1998–2002, the saber-intensity leaders were the New York Yankees, Boston, and Oakland (although their scores were practically identical.) During 2003–2007, the top three remained the same with the Yankees sliding below Boston and Oakland. Notably, during this period, the Tampa Bay Rays were in twenty-ninth place in the ranking. After the 2005 season, the Rays were purchased by Stu Sternberg. Sternberg brought in an Ivy-educated, investment banking team of executives and Andrew Friedman as GM and began to rebuild the team. The Rays rose from next-to-last to first place in the SI ranking during 2008–2011.

It is also notable that the A's slid from the top three down to tenth during 2008–11. This is consistent with our observation that Billy Beane appeared to switch strategies as formerly undervalued skills became fully valued. It bears noting as well that the A's surprising first-place divisional finish in 2012 is marked by a reemphasis on saber-intensity: in 2012, the A's ranked second in *obp*, third in *der*, and fourth in *iso* among all major league teams (and twelfth in *fip*).

Our next step is to see if the teams that had high SI scores in particular years also had high winning percentages in those years. To do this, however, we must first adjust for the fact that some teams benefitted from much higher payrolls than other teams. We do this by first estimating the impact of payroll (PAY) on win percentage (WPCT). PAY is considered as each team's payroll relative to the average major league payroll in each year. Because we expect there to be some diminishing returns to higher and higher payrolls, we estimate the following equation, again for the years 1985–2011:

Table 18. Top Three Teams, Average Saber-Intensity (SI) by Period

1992–1997		1998–2002		2003–2007		2008–2011	
Atlanta	1.0283	Yankees	1.0207	Boston	1.0208	Tampa Bay	1.0229
Baltimore	1.0162	Boston	1.0206	Oakland	1.0200	Boston	1.0163
Montreal	1.0117	Oakland	1.0204	Yankees	1.0145	Yankees	1.0158

$$WPCT = f(PAY, PAY^2)$$

The R^2 from this regression is 0.222, meaning that PAY and PAY^2 together explain 22.2 percent of the variance in win percentage, or that nonpayroll factors explain 77.8 percent. This result, of course, leaves ample margin for the influence of good scouting, good sabermetrics, good health, good chemistry, good managing, and good luck.[21]

The portion of win percentage that is not explained by the payroll factors is known as the residuals. To understand how the residual for each team in each year is generated, consider the Tampa Bay Rays in 2008. The estimated equation of wins on payrolls is Win Pct = 0.397+ 0.117 PAY − 0.012 PAY^2. The Rays spent about $51 million that season, which represented about 53 percent of the league average payroll. Using the equation above, this leads to the estimate that the Rays would have a 2008 win percentage of .455, which translates to about 74 wins. Their actual win percentage was .599 (97 wins). In this case, the Rays have a positive residual of .144 in 2008. Another way of looking at it is that .144 was that part of the Rays win percentage that was not explained by the Rays payroll.

Our next step is to see if teams' sabermetric intensity score is correlated to the teams' residuals in this win percentage regression. Specifically, we estimate the equation,

$$Residuals = f(SI),$$

for the entire period, 1985–2011. Our saber-intensity index explains 36.7 percent of the variance of the residuals; that is, SI explains just over one-third of that portion of team success that is not explained by team payroll.

$$Residual\ WPCT = -2.845 + 2.844\ SI \quad R^2 = 0.367$$

Viewed differently, for every .01 points that the SI[22] index increases, a team's win percentage increases by .028 points, or by roughly 4.5 games.

This result appears to give a ringing endorsement to sabermetrics. As a simple illustration, if a team can hire a corps of three statistical analysts for, say, $200,000 and thereby raise its sabermetric intensity from the average 1.00 to 1.01 (or by one percent), it would be equivalent to signing a player with a WAR of 4.5.[23] Such a player is likely to cost over $15 million. Indeed, on average, baseball teams appear to pay approximately $4 million per win on the free agent market. At today's prices, hiring a sabermetrician, or two, or three, is a steal.

An important caveat is that the low-hanging fruit—such as using OBP instead of BA—has already been picked. To be as productive going forward, tomorrow's sabermetricians will have to be smarter than their predecessors— and they are likely to cost more.[24] Still, they probably won't be as expensive as Alex Rodriguez per unit of output.

One more word of caution: as in most rapidly growing new fields, lots of people want to get in on the action. Before standards and procedures are developed for credentializing the would-be practitioners, this dynamic produces its share of charlatans, selling their supposed sabermetric skills to unwitting GMs. They usually come in the form of outside consultants with simple, yet flawed, statistical models. Sabermetrics doesn't work automatically; the right people have to be employed.

Conclusion

Sabermetrics, among other things, purports to quantify the value of players and their skills. In this chapter, we have attempted to develop a methodology to quantify the value of sabermetrics, or more precisely, the contribution that properly applying sabermetric insights makes to team performance. We do this in the spirit of initiating a line of inquiry, rather than presenting a final appraisal. Our initial findings are instructive and encouraging. Sabermetrics can add significant value.

Several qualifications are in order. First, like others, we have reified sabermetrics, but sabermetrics is not a static thing. It is a process that involves careful analysis of data. Sometimes the data is numerical, and sometimes it is visual. Increasingly, the cutting edge of sabermetric analysis seems to be focused on defense. Many of the new approaches to defense involve video analysis.

Thus, the saber-analyst more and more is using eyesight to observe play on the field—just like the scout. Meanwhile, scouts are assimilating many of the new metrics in their standard toolbox. The result is that much of the work of the sabermetrician and the scout is being integrated. As the functions merge, not only does it become more difficult to assess saber-intensity, but it is likely that a new paradigm for player evaluation is evolving that is multidimensional. Even as this happens, however, there will be a growing need for more sophisticated statistical analysis and programming skills to parse and process the mountains of new data that overwhelm many front offices.

Second, as old market inefficiencies disappear and the search for new ones continues, what really distinguishes one MLB front office from another is intelligence. Intelligent executives are more likely to explore new terrain and less likely to be threatened by innovative, more productive methods. They are also more able to identify what is important and what is superfluous. The consistently high scores on the saber-intensity index for the Atlanta Braves in the 1990s reflect not the explicit adoption of saber techniques, but the clear recognition of the importance of defense and pitching by Stan Kasten and John Schuerholz, the hiring of top scouts, and an effective player development system.[25]

While the Oakland A's reemergence as a competitive team in 2012 may be partly due to a renewed emphasis on saber-savvy metrics, it also reflects front office intelligence. The A's have been expanding, rather than contracting, their scouting budget in recent years. Billy Beane says that it is the A's commitment to statistical analysis that led them to increase the scouting budget. Beane elaborates: "What defines a good scout? Finding out information that other people can't. Getting to know the kid. Getting to know the family. There's just some things you have to find out in person."[26]

Almost by definition, baseball players who make it to the minor leagues are loaded with physical talent. A player's character is often the key factor that distinguishes him from others. Nate Silver breaks down a player's character traits this way: his work ethic, his concentration and focus, his competitiveness and self-confidence, his ability to manage stress, and his humility.[27] If a scout can identify these skills, then he is making a major contribution to team success.

Silver goes on assert: "If a team's forecasting is exceptionally good, perhaps it can pay $10 million a year for a player whose real value is $12 million. But if its scouting is really good, it might be paying the same player $400,000."[28] While Silver's example may be atypical in its magnitude, the direction of his claim is on the mark.

While Michael Lewis emphasizes the conflict between scouts and saber-metricians, smart baseball executives today know that there is no reason to tie one hand behind their backs. There is no sense in arbitrarily limiting the amount of information you gather. The trick is to parse and process the infor-mation effectively—a lesson that all companies have to learn.

APPENDIX

THE EXPECTED RUN MATRIX

At various points in this book we have referred to the Expected Run Matrix. As we indicated in the Preface, there are eight possible configurations of the baserunners in baseball (two possibilities for each of the three bases), and three possibilities for the number of outs in an inning. Thus, at any given point in an inning, the game can be classified as being in exactly one of twenty-four possible states. For example, at the beginning of each inning, the state is: nobody on, nobody out. Later, we might be in the state: runners on second and third, two outs. It is quite useful to associate with each of these twenty-four states, an estimate of the expected number of runs that an average team will score in the remainder of the inning. For the state (nobody on, nobody out), that value is simply the average number of runs scored per inning, which for the years 1985–2011 was 0.510. In contrast, if runners are on second and third with two outs, then the expected number of runs scored in the inning is 0.378. Obviously, these values are approximations of unknown quantities, since in a real game there are dozens of variables for which we haven't accounted. Nevertheless, knowing the expected run values for each state has proven to be an extremely useful framework for sabermetric analysis.

It is important to note that the Expected Run Matrix is not static. That is, the values can change considerably during different eras, when, for whatever reason, the run scoring environment is different. In Table 19, we present the Expected Run Matrix for 1982–1985 alongside the corresponding matrix for 1997–1999. Note how increasing the number of outs always decreases the run expectation, while increasing the numbers of baserunners always increases run expectation.

To illustrate, observe that with a runner on first and nobody out, a successful sacrifice bunt that advances the runner to second would result in a net

Table 19. Expected Run Matrix for 1982–1985 and 1997–1999

	1982–1985			1997–1999		
Bases \ Outs	*0*	*1*	*2*	*0*	*1*	*2*
Bases empty	0.482	0.254	0.098	0.552	0.296	0.114
Runner on first	0.866	0.505	0.215	0.939	0.571	0.242
Runner on second	1.115	0.667	0.321	1.197	0.707	0.343
Runners on first and second	1.459	0.894	0.421	1.540	0.968	0.457
Runner on third	1.361	0.963	0.368	1.427	0.999	0.376
Runners on first and third	1.734	1.187	0.479	1.879	1.214	0.527
Runners on second and third	2.006	1.400	0.598	2.044	1.430	0.594
Bases loaded	2.294	1.568	0.749	2.364	1.634	0.784

loss of 0.866 – 0.667 = 0.199 expected runs in the early 1980s, but a decrease of 0.939 – 0.707 = 0.232 expected runs in the late 1990s. The matrix is one methodology that is used for detecting the average incremental impact of different strategies and batter outcomes during the course of a game.

MODELING THE EFFECTIVENESS OF
SABERMETRIC STATISTICS

In this section we describe our methodology for modeling the extent of effective implementation of sabermetrics in Major League Baseball and the resulting impact on team performance. Our approach has three main components:

1. We build a model for the winning percentage of a team as a function of their payroll.
2. We construct metrics that are designed to indicate the influence of sabermetrics on the team's composition and performance.
3. We examine the relationship between the residuals from the model from part 1 with the metrics constructed in part 2.

The presence of meaningful associations between the residuals from the first model and the sabermetric intensity metrics is a method for detecting the presence of and quantifying the impact of sabermetrics among clubs.

Modeling Team Performance as a Function of Payroll

Our first task is to understand the role of team payroll upon performance. Our data set contains performance statistics obtained from Retrosheet,[1] as well as team year-end payroll data (in nominal dollars) obtained from MLB's Labor Relations department and used with permission. The data contains complete information on all major league clubs (768 team-seasons) from 1985 to 2011.

Next, we want to contextualize the payroll data. We do this by defining PAY as the share of a team's payroll relative to the league average share, which is by definition the total amount spent divided by the number of clubs. Note

Table 20. Relationship Between Win Percentage and Payroll, with Team Fixed Effects

	Estimate	Standard Error	t-statistic	Pr(> |t|)
(Intercept)	0.3909	0.0202	19.36	0.00
PAY	0.1261	0.0274	4.61	0.00
PAY^2	−0.0125	0.0120	−1.04	0.29
R^2	0.29			

that this correction is necessary, since the number of clubs has not remained constant over the time period in question.[2] Thus, PAY implicitly controls for both U.S. inflation and for baseball salary inflation simultaneously. In order to characterize the relationship between payroll and winning percentage, we run a regression model for winning percentage (WPCT) as a function of PAY, PAY^2, and team fixed effects.[3] The details from this model are shown in Table 20.

Our model satisfies the conditions for multiple linear regression well. Although the quadratic term was not statistically significant at the 5 percent level, we chose to include it so as to incorporate the desirable notion of diminishing returns to payroll. Moreover, analysis of the residuals favored the model that included the quadratic term.

Measuring Sabermetric Intensity

In the previous section we described a model for a team's winning percentage (WPCT) as a function of its relative share of league payroll (equivalently, the ratio of their payroll to the league average). In this section, we develop a series of metrics designed to measure the intensity of a team's sabermetric practice. That is, we will attempt to quantify the extent to which the on-field performance of a team reflects sabermetric thinking.

In what follows, we develop relatively simple metrics that we hope will capture some element of sabermetric practice on the part of front offices. Generally, our approach to building metrics that measure sabermetric intensity is to examine the ratio of a saber-savvy metric to a more traditional performance metric. In this respect, we are not advocating for any of these particular metrics, but merely suggesting that they might be popular among either traditionalists or sabermetricians. In practice, this process involves several steps:

1. Apply ballpark corrections to performance data
2. Compute the ratio of each statistic to the league average in that year
3. Compute the ratio of the sabermetric statistic to the traditional statistic

In the resulting metrics, a higher score reflects more saber-intensity, i.e., better performance in the sabermetric statistics relative to the traditional statistic.

Step 1: Ballpark Corrections

First, we have to adjust our raw performance data for ballpark conditions. We have to chosen to do this using the ballpark factors provided by Sean Lahman[4] (appropriately scaled). These park factors reflect inflation in *runs* that are attributable to a specific park. For example, the batting and pitching *run park factors* (BPF and PPF, respectively) for Fenway Park in 2004 were 1.06 and 1.05, respectively. This suggests that Fenway Park inflated run scoring by about 5 to 6 percent, relative to a league average park. Simply dividing each statistic by this number would result in statistics that were correlated to the park factor. In contrast, the notion of correcting for ballpark is to *remove* the component of a statistic that is attributable to the park. Thus, we correct for park by building a simple linear model for each statistic as a function of the park factor, and then adding the resulting residuals of that regression to the league average. This procedure removes nearly all correlation between the park factor and the park-corrected statistics.[5]

Step 2: Relative to League Average

After correcting for ballpark, we want to correct for the run scoring of the time period. This has changed considerably over the time period in question, as demonstrated in Figure 13. We thus normalize the metric relative to the average value of that statistic for each league in each year.

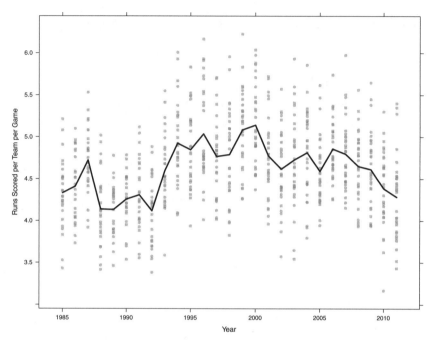

Figure 13. Runs Scored per Game, 1985–2011
Each dot represents one team in one season, with the league average shown as a line. It
is apparent that run scoring was at its highest level during the late 1990s, and that it has
fallen sharply in recent years.

To illustrate the nature of these corrections, we compare OBP, park-factored OBP (OBP.pf), and relative park-factored OBP (rel.OBP.pf) by franchise over this time period in Table 21 below. Note how the park factors affect
a few teams in extreme ways (e.g., Colorado, San Diego), while interpreting
the statistics relative to the league average improves the standing of the National League teams considerably.

On the pitching side, we see similar changes. While teams like the Dodgers and Mets have low ERAs overall, after correcting for their pitching-
friendly ballparks, their standings decrease. Conversely, teams like Texas and
Colorado that play in hitter-friendly ballparks move up in the rankings.

Table 21. Effect of Park Factor Adjustments on OBP, 1985–2011

Team	OBP	OBP.pf	rel.OBP.pf
New York Yankees	0.348	0.352	1.040
Boston	0.348	0.349	1.033
St. Louis	0.333	0.330	1.020
Cleveland	0.337	0.341	1.009
Colorado	0.344	0.334	1.009
Philadelphia	0.331	0.326	1.008
Houston	0.329	0.326	1.008
Oakland	0.335	0.340	1.007
San Francisco	0.327	0.325	1.005
New York Mets	0.327	0.325	1.004
Atlanta	0.330	0.325	1.004
San Diego	0.325	0.324	1.002
Texas	0.337	0.338	1.001
Cincinnati	0.329	0.324	1.001
Florida	0.330	0.331	0.999
Los Angeles Dodgers	0.324	0.323	0.998
Minnesota	0.334	0.337	0.998
Seattle	0.333	0.337	0.997
Baltimore	0.332	0.336	0.995
Chicago White Sox	0.333	0.336	0.993
Detroit	0.331	0.335	0.992
Milwaukee	0.329	0.331	0.990
Los Angeles Angels	0.331	0.335	0.990
Toronto	0.332	0.334	0.989
Pittsburgh	0.323	0.319	0.988
Chicago Cubs	0.324	0.319	0.986
Washington	0.322	0.318	0.983
Arizona	0.329	0.326	0.983
Tampa Bay	0.327	0.333	0.980
Kansas City	0.326	0.329	0.974

Step 3: Construction of Sabermetric Intensity Metrics

The central idea behind our sabermetric intensity metrics is to examine the ratio of a statistic that likely reflects sabermetric adherence relative to a traditional metric that purports to measure that same quantity. For example, adherents of sabermetrics are more likely to value OBP over batting average

Table 22. Effect of Park Factor Adjustments on ERA and FIP, 1985–2011

Team	ERA	ERA.pf	rel.ERA.pf	FIP	FIP.pf	rel.FIP.pf
Atlanta	3.774	3.562	0.921	3.388	3.341	0.973
Boston	4.228	4.264	0.937	3.460	3.477	0.968
LA Dodgers	3.699	3.675	0.939	3.380	3.366	0.980
Toronto	4.222	4.345	0.952	3.520	3.552	0.989
Arizona	4.274	4.128	0.962	3.495	3.463	0.986
LA Angels	4.218	4.398	0.963	3.544	3.586	0.998
NY Mets	3.868	3.791	0.971	3.427	3.403	0.990
Chi. White Sox	4.296	4.431	0.973	3.553	3.587	0.999
St. Louis	3.948	3.808	0.974	3.476	3.441	1.002
NY Yankees	4.243	4.427	0.978	3.499	3.541	0.987
Oakland	4.193	4.484	0.981	3.534	3.596	1.001
Washington	4.046	3.866	0.984	3.475	3.433	0.999
Houston	3.978	3.868	0.997	3.437	3.407	0.992
San Francisco	3.968	3.906	1.003	3.477	3.456	1.006
Minnesota	4.483	4.593	1.007	3.550	3.579	0.997
Seattle	4.398	4.592	1.009	3.555	3.599	1.002
Kansas City	4.542	4.625	1.013	3.556	3.581	0.997
Milwaukee	4.379	4.410	1.018	3.571	3.588	1.010
Chicago Cubs	4.221	3.963	1.018	3.500	3.445	1.003
Cincinnati	4.231	3.990	1.020	3.536	3.484	1.014
Cleveland	4.440	4.626	1.021	3.540	3.583	0.998
Philadelphia	4.174	3.968	1.023	3.511	3.465	1.009
San Diego	4.010	4.007	1.023	3.468	3.457	1.006
Florida	4.336	4.389	1.032	3.506	3.504	1.003
Texas	4.660	4.707	1.032	3.591	3.610	1.005
Tampa Bay	4.686	4.972	1.048	3.633	3.676	1.024
Colorado	5.029	4.473	1.054	3.647	3.537	1.013
Pittsburgh	4.309	4.132	1.058	3.519	3.478	1.013
Detroit	4.645	4.826	1.059	3.633	3.675	1.023
Baltimore	4.627	4.818	1.062	3.627	3.671	1.023

(BA), so proponents of sabermetrics are likely to have higher ratios of OBP/ BA than teams that value traditional metrics.

To illustrate, the following scatterplot shows the relationship between relative OBP and relative BA, with Oakland's teams highlighted in black. Thus, in considering a team's on base ability, we define *onbase* to be this ratio.

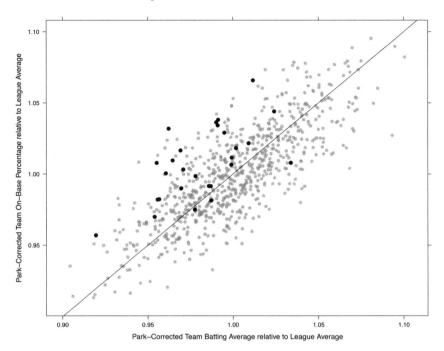

Figure 14. Scatterplot of *onbase*, 1985–2011
Each dot represents one team in one season, with the horizontal coordinate given by
the team's park-corrected batting average relative to league, and the vertical coordinate
given by the corresponding figure for OBP. The black diagonal represents a ratio of 1:1.
Oakland is shown with dark black dots. The fact that these points lie above the diagonal
in all but three seasons reflects an emphasis on OBP relative to batting average.

While this is an admittedly crude measurement of sabermetric adherence, it does implicitly control for the quality of players that a team is able to
put on the field. That is, while the Royals' OBP may not keep pace with that
of the Yankees, there is a priori no reason to believe that their ratio of OBP/
BA should not be as high.

It will likely come as little surprise that Oakland dominates the list of
teams that score highly in this metric, claiming five of the top twenty spots
over the period 1985 to 2011.

We construct similar metrics that value each of the basic elements of baseball: getting on base, hitting for power (*iso*), pitching (*fip*), fielding (*der*), baserunning (*brun*), and sacrifice bunting frequency (*sacbunt*). For all of these

Table 23. Top Twenty Team-Years in OBP/BA (onbase)

Year	Team	WPCT	rel.AVG.pf	rel.OBP.pf	onbase
1999	**Oakland**	**0.537**	**0.962**	**1.032**	**1.072**
1991	Detroit	0.519	0.945	1.008	1.067
2010	Tampa Bay	0.593	0.961	1.024	1.065
1985	LA Angels	0.556	0.960	1.018	1.061
1990	Baltimore	0.472	0.956	1.013	1.060
2006	Boston	0.531	0.967	1.024	1.059
2006	**Oakland**	**0.574**	**0.955**	**1.008**	**1.055**
1992	NY Mets	0.444	0.932	0.983	1.054
1992	**Oakland**	**0.593**	**1.012**	**1.066**	**1.053**
2003	NY Yankees	0.623	1.019	1.073	1.053
2011	NY Yankees	0.599	1.000	1.053	1.053
2000	Seattle	0.562	0.990	1.042	1.052
1986	LA Angels	0.568	0.980	1.029	1.050
1991	**Oakland**	**0.519**	**0.969**	**1.017**	**1.049**
2004	NY Yankees	0.623	0.999	1.048	1.049
1997	Florida	0.568	0.999	1.048	1.049
1989	Detroit	0.364	0.933	0.978	1.048
2011	Tampa Bay	0.562	0.966	1.013	1.048
1994	Detroit	0.461	0.972	1.019	1.048
2001	**Oakland**	**0.630**	**0.991**	**1.038**	**1.047**

metrics, the league average in any given season is 1 by definition. We believe that while these sabermetric intensity metrics are far from perfect, they do capture something meaningful.

Inefficiencies Exploited by Sabermetrics

We saw previously that Oakland had the largest positive team effect in our payroll model. In this context we want to understand the deviations from the general relationship between winning percentage and payroll, so we compute the model without team fixed effects, and later investigate the relationship of those residuals for patterns with respect to our composite saber-intensity (SI) metric. The equation tested below is WPCT = f(PAY, PAY^2).

Oakland, St. Louis, Atlanta, the Chicago White Sox, Minnesota, and Florida have the largest average residuals.

Table 24. The Relationship Between Win Percentage and Payroll, Without Team Fixed Effects

	Estimate	Standard Error	t value	Pr(> |t|)
(Intercept)	0.3966	0.0128	30.89	0
PAY	0.1165	0.0230	5.07	0
PAY^2	-0.0116	0.0098	-1.18	0.2368
R^2	0.222			

Building a Composite Sabermetric Index

Our goal here is to build a single index that will measure sabermetric intensity. To do this, we need weights for each of the elements of saber-intensity. A reasonable choice for those weights is the normalized coefficients from a double-log model for WPCT as a function of the sabermetric variables that we are tracking. That model is presented below. Since the baserunning statistic can be negative, we transform it so that it is always positive. The natural log of WPCT is the dependent variable.

The value of these coefficients gives us a sense of the relative impact that each has on WPCT. Note that while a team's fielding metric (DER) appears to have the largest impact upon WPCT, each of the six terms has a statistically significant effect at the 10 percent level or better.

In order to use these coefficients as weights, we drop the coefficient for the intercept term, take their absolute values, and then normalize them.

Table 25. Double Log Model to Weight Components of SI Index

	Estimate	Standard Error	t value	Pr(> |t|)
(Intercept)	5.6072	0.1173	47.79	0
log(OBP)	1.7419	0.0689	25.27	0
log(ISO)	0.2749	0.0192	14.3	0
log(FIP)	-2.1363	0.0674	-31.71	0
log(DER)	3.1852	0.1421	22.41	0
log(baserunning)	0.0057	0.0034	1.7	0.0888
log(sacbunt)	-0.0148	0.0085	-1.73	0.0837
R^2	0.80			

Table 26. Final Component Weights in SI Index

log(OBP)	0.2367
log(ISO)	0.0374
log(FIP)	0.2903
log(DER)	0.4328
log(brun)	0.0008
log(sacbunt)	0.0020

This suggests that roughly 43 percent of our sabermetric index will consist of a team's fielding metric (DER). These weights are then applied to our six saber-intensity elements to generate our composite index of saber-intensity (SI). The results for the top thirty teams in SI between 1985 and 2011 are presented in Table 17 in Chapter 7.

When we regress the residuals from the WPCT and payroll regression on our saber-intensity index, the results are presented in Table 27.

Note that since the average team has an SI of 1, the predicted WPCT residual (the expected impact of all factors other than payroll) is zero for the average team.[6] It is worth reiterating that there is no reason to believe, independent of sabermetrics, that a team with a high sabermetric index would be more successful than their payroll would indicate. Yet the regression model above shows that our sabermetric index explains nearly 37 percent of the variation in team winning percentage that is not explained by payroll.

Table 27. Relationship of Win Percentage and Team Saber-Intensity (SI)

	Estimate	Std. Error	t value	$Pr(>|t|)$
(Intercept)	-2.8447	0.1349	-21.08	0
SI	2.8438	0.1349	21.09	0
R^2	0.367			

MODELING THE SHIFTING INEFFICIENCIES
IN MLB LABOR MARKETS

In this section we describe how we modeled our test for the morphing inefficiencies in baseball's labor market. Our approach is an extension of the one employed by Hakes and Sauer in 2006.[7]

There are two main components to this procedure. First, we construct a model for team performance in terms of simple performance metrics. In this manner, we gain an understanding of what skills translate into team success. Second, we construct a model for how those skills are compensated on the labor market. Market inefficiencies are reflected in the differences in the estimates between these two models.

Hakes and Sauer identified three largely orthogonal qualities that reflect on-field performance for both batters and pitchers: Eye (walks plus hit by pitch per plate appearance), Bat (batting average), and Power (slugging percentage divided by batting average). Since there is a natural equality to the way in which a team's offense and defense contribute to their success, the Hakes and Sauer model constrains the coefficients such that the Eye of a team's hitters makes an equal contribution to the Eye of the opposing team (EyeA). The dependent variable is team winning percentage above .500. Thus, the full model is:

$$\text{WPCT} - 0.5 = \beta_0 + \beta_1 (\text{Eye} - \text{EyeA}) + \beta_2 (\text{Bat} - \text{BatA}) + \beta_3 (\text{Power} - \text{PowerA})$$

In Table 28, we present the coefficients, standard errors, and R^2s for this model applied to different periods of time. Our results largely correspond with those presented by Hakes and Sauer, although with the benefit of hindsight, we are able to draw more nuanced conclusions.

Table 28. Effect of Hitting Skills on WPCT

	1985–2012	1985–1997	1998–2002	2003–2007	2008–2012
Constant	0.500	0.500	0.500	0.500	0.500
Eye	1.713	1.862	1.555	1.758	1.419
	(0.081)	(0.136)	(0.167)	(0.157)	(0.217)
Power	0.264	0.272	0.219	0.260	0.319
	(0.016)	(0.027)	(0.031)	(0.034)	(0.039)
Bat	3.005	2.907	3.266	2.911	3.087
	(0.074)	(0.119)	(0.150)	(0.162)	(0.174)
B(Eye)/B(Bat)	0.570	0.641	0.476	0.604	0.460
B(Eye)/B(Power)	6.497	6.839	7.117	6.747	4.448
N	798	348	150	150	150
R^2	0.814	0.773	0.882	0.827	0.808

Note: The standard errors are in parentheses below the estimated coefficients.

The second component of this evaluation is to model how these skills are valued on the labor market. Here, we construct a model for the natural log of the salary of an individual player as a function of his performance in these three statistics in the previous season. Control variables are added for plate appearances, free agency and arbitration eligibility, indicator variables for catchers and infielders, and fixed effects for each year. Only players with 130 plate appearances are included. The results are shown in Table 29.

Table 29. The Effect of Hitting Skills on Player Salary

	1986–2012	1985–1997	1998–2002	2003–2007	2008–2012
Eye	2.000	1.667	1.434	2.827	2.782
	(0.210)	(0.287)	(0.417)	(0.521)	(0.562)
Power	0.667	0.611	0.745	0.731	0.578
	(0.034)	(0.049)	(0.070)	(0.086)	(0.086)
Bat	3.672	3.402	3.910	4.274	3.828
	(0.235)	(0.334)	(0.473)	(0.614)	(0.579)
B(Eye)/B(Power)	3.000	2.727	1.926	3.869	4.815
B(Eye)/B(Bat)	0.545	0.490	0.367	0.614	0.727
N	8824	3668	1748	1707	1701
R^2	0.771	0.735	0.787	0.722	0.719

Note: The standard errors are in parentheses below the estimated coefficients.

The foregoing represents our basic approach. Various permutations in the modeling were attempted, including taking logs of each of the independent variables. Notable results are discussed in Chapter 7.

NOTES

Preface

1. To be sure, Taylor was concerned with other elements of workplace design and control as well. See, for instance, Charles Wrege and Amedeo Perroni, "Taylor's Pig-Tale: A Historical Analysis of Frederick W. Taylor's Pig-Iron Experiments," *Academy of Management Journal* 17, no. 1 (March 1974), 6–27, and Harry Braverman, *Labor and Monopoly Capital* (New York: Monthly Review Press, 1974).

2. Prior to the Industrial Revolution, some of the earliest uses of measurement and numbers were attached to sport. For an excellent discussion of the historical evolution of measurement in sports, see Allen Guttmann, *From Ritual to Record: The Nature of Modern Sports* (New York: Columbia University Press, 1978).

Chapter 1. Revisiting *Moneyball*

1. Hyperbole is equally present in the 2012 anti-*Moneyball* movie, *Trouble with the Curve*, wherein the sabermetricians are portrayed as unlikeable buffoons and the scouts as insightful mavens. As with *Moneyball*, *Trouble with the Curve*'s emotional appeal is largely driven by a father-daughter relationship.

2. Scott Sherman, "Rethinking America's Pastime: The Paul DePodesta Story," *Harvard Crimson*, May 5, 2012.

3. Also see, for instance, Michael Lewis, *Moneyball* (New York: W. W. Norton, 2003), p. 256.

4. See, for one, Alan Schwarz, *The Numbers Game: Baseball's Lifelong Fascination with Statistics* (New York: St. Martin's Press, 2004), p. 75, citing Lindsey's 1959 article in the journal *Operations Research*.

5. See, for example, Tom Tango, Mitchel G. Lichtman, and Andrew E. Dolphin, *The Book: Playing the Percentages in Baseball* (Washington, D.C.: Potomac Books, 2007), chapter 11. For further reading see J. Click, "What if Rickey Henderson Had Pete Incaviglia's Legs?" in *Baseball Between the Numbers: Why Everything You Know About the Game Is Wrong* (New York: Basic Books, 2007), chapter 4-1, 112–126; and B. Baumer, J. Piette, and B. Null, "Parsing the Relationship Between Baserunning and Batting Abilities Within Lineups," *Journal of Quantitative Analysis in Sports* 8, no. 2 (2012).

6. This average applies to the years 1985–2011.

7. Even if one took out the contributions by Johnny Damon and Jason Giambi, the A's OBP in 2001 and 2000 was .331 and .346, respectively. That is, without their contributions, the 2002 A's still only exceeded the OBP in one of the two previous years. Nonetheless, the point is that Beane set out to at least replace the lost OBP of these two players and he failed to do so.

8. Lewis, *Moneyball*, p. 248.

9. For now, suffice it to note that WAR suffers from a variety of deficiencies. Among other issues, different authors and websites have different definitions of WAR. The one we employ here is from Baseball-Reference.com, and, hence, more precisely should be designated as either bWAR or rWAR. We use WAR on occasion because it is standard in the sabermetric vernacular and there are no comprehensive measures of player performance that are clearly superior.

10. See http://www.baseball-reference.com/teams/OAK/2002.shtml.

11. In Chapter 5, we discuss the barren state of error bounds for WAR. In the case of the 2002 A's, every pitcher other than the five mentioned above had a WAR between −0.5 and 0.5, which even WAR proponents acknowledge is within the margin of error.

12. Of these pitchers, Zito is perhaps the only question mark because he was not a particularly hard thrower and Lewis suggests that only a team eschewing the traditional measures of pitching talent would have drafted him. However, if Zito were a diamond in the rough that only the sabermetric eyes of Billy Beane could spot, then there would have been little reason to waste a first-round (ninth overall) pick on him in 1999. The A's could have waited until the second, third, or a later round to draft Zito. The fact of the matter is that Zito was well-scouted and highly touted; see, for instance, Sheldon Hirsch and Alan Hirsch, *The Beauty of Short Hops* (Jefferson, N.C.: McFarland, 2011), p. 18. Indeed, in 1998 the Texas Rangers drafted Zito in the third round, though Zito didn't sign and returned to finish his college career at USC, where he was a first-team All-America selection by *USA Today, Baseball Weekly, Collegiate Baseball*, and *Baseball America*. With a 12–3 record, a 3.28 ERA, and 154 strikeouts in 113⅔ innings, Zito was named Pac-10 Pitcher of the Year in 1999.

13. Lewis, *Moneyball*, p. 231.

14. Lewis appears to misrepresent the speed of another pitcher's velocity. In discussing Jason Grimsley's pitching prowess in 2002 Lewis writes (p. 260): "With a pitcher like Grimsley you always know what you'll be getting: 96-mph heat." Grimsley may have reached that velocity occasionally at the beginning of his career, but arm injuries and time conspired to make him a slower sinkerball pitcher by 2002. According to data on Fangraphs.com, for instance, his fastball in 2002 came in at 93 miles per hour.

15. ERA+ is a pitcher's earned run average, adjusted for ballpark factors, relative to the league average. WHIP stands for walks and hits per inning pitched. WHIP, while increasingly used, is deficient in that it does not adjust for fielding and factors of chance.

16. In 2001, the A's drafted Bobby Crosby, Jeremy Bonderman, Neal Cotts, Dan

Johnson, and Mike Wood, all of whom played at least three years in the big leagues. It is hard to think of this output from one draft as a disaster. According to our model detailed below, the A's earned 3.2 WAR beyond what would have been expected in this draft. Unfortunately for the A's, about two-thirds of that was accumulated by Bonderman while wearing a Tigers uniform.

17. All of these ten at bats were with the A's, and during September call-ups at that. It is not likely that any other team would have called him up even for such a short cup of coffee. Some in the baseball industry even suggested that Beane called him up to increase the number of major leaguers he drafted in 2002.

18. Blanton has had a solid major league career. He was the 24th pick in the 2002 draft. The 25th pick that year was the Giants' all-star pitcher Matt Cain. Teahen was not a bad 39th pick. He was used to facilitate a useful trade for the team and he played seven years in the majors. Five picks after him, however, at 44th, Cincinnati selected first baseman Joey Votto, who became the 2010 National League MVP.

19. Lewis, *Moneyball*, p. 116.

20. We chose 220 players so as to include Colamarino, the 218th pick in the 2002 draft. Both models were fit to a negative exponential distribution, where the response variable was WAR, and the explanatory variable was the overall draft pick slot. The only difference between the two models is whether minor league players were assigned a WAR of 0, or excluded from the data set. Our model is largely consistent with the findings reported in Rany Jazayerli, "Doctoring the Numbers: The Draft," *Baseball Prospectus*, May 13, 2005. http://www.baseballprospectus.com/article.php?articleid=4026.

21. To be more precise, the net WAR of 6.4 earned by the A's in the 2002 draft ranks in the seventy-first percentile among the 464 team drafts between 1990 and 2005.

22. In this case the A's net WAR of 2.0 ranks in the 65th percentile.

23. Lewis, *Moneyball*, pp. 103–106.

24. Lewis, *Moneyball*, p. 20.

25. Lewis, *Moneyball*, p. 109.

26. Lewis, *Moneyball*, p. 109.

27. Lewis, *Moneyball*, p. 17.

28. Bonderman also started Game 4 of the 2006 ALCS against the A's, leaving a tie game in the seventh inning. The Tigers scored three runs in the ninth to sweep the A's out of the playoffs.

29. Lewis, *Moneyball*, p. 112.

30. Bryan Bullington (1) and Jeff Francis (9) were college players. Adam Loewen (4) was drafted out of junior college.

31. Lewis, *Moneyball*, p. 112.

32. Of the thirty players selected in the first round of the 2002 draft (one of whom did not sign that year), the fifteen high school players have accumulated nearly 63 percent of the cumulative major league service time and 76 percent of the WAR. Only one

of the five players who never played in the major leagues was a high schooler (Chris Gruler at 3), while two others were selected by the A's (McCurdy and Ben Fritz) and a third was on their list (Bobby Brownlie). To be fair, Swisher and Blanton are probably the two most accomplished college players selected (Jeff Francis, Jeremy Guthrie, and Joe Saunders have also had decent careers), but the list of high school players is loaded with superstars (B. J. Upton, Fielder, Greinke, Matt Cain, Cole Hamels, Kazmir) and players who have had careers approaching those of Swisher and Blanton (Denard Span, Jeff Francoeur, Khalil Greene, James Loney).

33. Schwarz, *The Numbers Game*, pp. 124–126. James believed, as did Chadwick and many others, that the commonly used "fielding percentage" failed to measure a fielder's ability to get to a batted ball. The range factor metric was an (ultimately flawed) early effort to rectify this deficiency.

34. Quoted in Schwarz, *The Numbers Game*, p. 34.

35. Arguably, Rickey acted even before this. One source has Rickey hiring Travis Hoke to do a statistical analysis of the St. Louis Cardinals in the 1930s. See Dayn Perry, "Extra Innings: Can Stats and Scouts Get Along?" in Jonah Keri (ed.), *Baseball Between the Numbers* (New York: Basic Books, 2006).

36. SLG is slugging percentage, where the numerator is the number of total bases on base hits divided by the number of at bats. That is, a single counts as one base, a double as two bases, a triple as three, and a home run as four.

37. Lindsey's baseball work was published in two articles in the journal *Operations Research* in 1959 and 1963.

38. Frank Deford, "Baseball Is Played All Wrong," *Sports Illustrated,* March 23, 1964, pp. 14–17.

39. Schwarz, *The Numbers Game*, and interview, June 22, 2012. Schwarz speculated that Earl Weaver was also aware of Cook's writings, both because of Deford's piece and because there were several articles in the Baltimore newspapers on Cook's work. Weaver, however, says that his approach was based entirely on his experience as a minor leaguer and learning from experimentation as a manager (interview, June 27, 2012). Lou Gorman also served as the assistant GM of the Orioles and the Mets, and was the farm director of the Kansas City Royals.

40. Also part of the Orioles (and Reds) system in the 1960s and 1970s was head scout Jim McLaughlin. McLaughlin had a systematic and statistical method for scouting players that included computerizing player data, using professional psychological testing methods to assess the makeup of each prospect, systematizing the measurement of scout performance, and employing physical testing to quantify each player's skills. See Kevin Kerrane, *Dollar Sign on the Muscle: The World of Baseball Scouting* (Lincoln, Neb.: Bison Books, 1999).

41. According to an article in SABR's *Baseball Research Journal*, "1977: When Earl Weaver Became Earl Weaver," Fall 2011, by Bryan Soderholm-Difatte, Weaver did not put his new philosophy fully into play until 1977.

42. Although Eric Walker has been out of baseball since the 1990s, he has continued to write about the game. Most notably, he maintains a website, steroids-and-baseball.com, in which he rants against the Mitchell Report on steroids prepared by the committee led by George Mitchell for the commissioner's office and avers that there is no statistical evidence linking steroid use to increased power in the game. For a critical discussion of Walker's statistical analysis, see A. Zimbalist, "Performance-Enhancing Drugs and Antidoping Policy in Major League Baseball," in Zimbalist (ed.), *Circling the Bases: Essays on the Challenges and Prospects of the Sports Industry* (Philadelphia: Temple University Press, 2011).

43. Lewis incorrectly states: "Palmer had written a book back in the 1960s revealing all this. The manuscript was still gathering dust on his desk when Bill James came along and created a market for it" (p. 80). Yet according to both Pete Palmer and John Thorn, there was no such book in the 1960s or the 1970s. There was just statistical work that Palmer had done. The book was written largely by John Thorn in the early 1980s.

44. Schwarz, *The Numbers Game*, pp. 220-225.

45. Interviews with Dan Duquette on June 11, 2012 and with Larry Lucchino on June 12, 2012.

46. Schwarz, *The Numbers Game*, p. 227.

47. Lewis also reminds the reader on p. 69: "The cause was the systematic search for new baseball knowledge."

48. Lewis, *Moneyball*, p. 14.

49. Lewis, *Moneyball*, p. 193.

50. The A's front office had conducted "a systematic scientific investigation of their sport." Lewis, *Moneyball*, p. xiv.

51. Lewis, *Moneyball*, p. 201.

52. Lewis's confusions do not end here. For instance, he both extols Beane's instilling a culture of patience at the plate throughout the A's minor league system and yet writes that Beane believed that plate "discipline can't be taught" (*Moneyball*, p. 148).

53. Lewis, *Moneyball*, p. xiv.

54. Lewis, *Moneyball*, p. 277.

55. Lewis, *Moneyball*, p. 277. Also see, Baseball-Reference.com on J. P. Ricciardi and Keith Law's commentary on Baseball Think Factory, September 15, 2011.

56. Of course, team payrolls rose between these periods, from an average median payroll of $60.5 million during 2000–2001 to $78.6 million during 2002–2009. So the Blue Jays' payroll rose slightly less than that of the average team, but Ricciardi's reported pledge was to decrease payroll in absolute terms.

57. Lewis, *Moneyball*, p. 122.

58. As perceptions catch up to realities and some market inefficiencies disappear, it is always possible that new market inefficiencies will emerge and the perspicacious GM will be able to stay one step ahead of the field and exploit these. Indeed, as we shall see, Beane's strategy does seem to have shifted over the years.

59. On p. 205, Lewis, in reference to the negotiations for the 2002 collective bargaining agreement (CBA), cites Beane as believing that the only way the draft pick compensation for free agents would be changed is if the players were to allow either a salary cap or team revenue sharing. In fact, baseball's modern revenue sharing system was introduced in the 1996 CBA, and by 2002, the amount of sharing from the rich to poor teams had grown to over $165 million. Beane must have known this, but Lewis should have known, too, given that he was writing a book about how to resolve MLB's competitive balance problem. Lewis commits a similar gaffe on p. 3 when he states that the players "had been granted free agency by a court of law." Free agency was granted by an internal baseball arbitrator, Peter Seitz, on December 21, 1975, in a sixty-one-page decision. The Seitz ruling was later upheld in a court of law.

60. The idealized standard deviation is a hypothetical concept that would apply under the assumption that all teams had equal talent and, therefore, a 0.5 chance of winning each game. The ratio shows how far the actual deviates from the idealized standard deviation. It is a useful metric for cross league and longitudinal comparisons.

61. The coefficient of variation is the standard deviation divided by the mean. It adjusts for the increase in average payrolls over time.

62. Frank and Murray are both quoted by Alan Schwarz in *The Numbers Game*, p. 131.

Chapter 2. The Growth and Application of Baseball Analytics Today

1. Lewis, *Moneyball*, pp. 89–90.

2. Lewis, *Moneyball*, p. 95.

3. S. T. Jensen, K. E. Shirley, and A. J. Wyner, "Bayesball: A Bayesian Hierarchical Model for Evaluating Fielding in Major League Baseball," *Annals of Applied Statistics*, 3, no. 2 (2009), pp. 491–520.

4. Of course, in those cases where a former baseball operations person is the team president, such as with the Cubs and Marlins, it is possible to think of this position as the third, instead of the second, post.

5. Scott Sherman, "Rethinking America's Pastime: The Paul DePodesta Story," *Harvard Crimson*, May 5, 2012.

6. Also not included in our count are consultants, because these relationships are nearly impossible to identify and unravel. However, such arrangements certainly exist. In early 2013, prominent sabermetrician Tom Tango signed an exclusive consulting services contract with Theo Epstein and the Chicago Cubs. (See Jon Greenberg, "Q&A: New Cubs 'Saberist' Tom Tango," ESPNChicago.com, January 30, 2013, http://espn.go.com/blog/chicago/cubs/post/_/id/14619/qa-new-cubs-saberist-tom-tango). But since we can't know the extent and depth of Tango's contribution, we felt it best to exclude all consultants.

7. Jim Duquette, personal communication via email, April 17, 2013.

8. Phillies GM Ruben Amaro observed: "Since I've been here, we don't have an in-house stats guy and I kind of feel we never will. We're not a statistics-driven organization

by any means." Doug Miller, "New Defensive Stats Starting to Catch On," *MLB.com*, January 11, 2010. Amaro publicly reconsidered his antithetical stance toward sabermetrics after the team's poor 2013 season, stating, "We may be looking to fortify some of our information with some more statistical analysis. We have to look at the way we do things and try to improve. . . . I'm not so stubborn that we can't try to do things a little bit different." Tyler Kepner, "Fresh Leadership for Stale Phillies," *New York Times*, August 26, 2013.

9. Personal communications.

10. For example, Karl Mueller's job title with the Brewers is director, video scouting and baseball research.

11. For example, Chris Long of the San Diego Padres has an M.A. in mathematics from Rutgers University, and was ABD (all but dissertation) in the Ph.D. program in statistics.

12. Keith Woolner of the Cleveland Indians has a M.S. in decision analysis from Stanford University.

13. Formerly, Jim Cassandro of the Arizona Diamondbacks would have qualified. One of the present authors, Ben Baumer, briefly would have been in this category with the New York Mets. Daniel Mack earned a Ph.D. in computer science before joining the Royals in 2013.

14. Lewis, *Moneyball*, p. 99.

15. While the book by Jonah Keri, *The Extra 2%: How Wall Street Strategies Took a Major League Baseball Team from Worst to First* (New York: Ballantine Books, 2011) appropriately calls attention to the innovative nature of the Tampa Bay Rays management, it misrepresents the substance of the Rays' management practices.

16. Lewis, *Moneyball*, p. 18.

17. Lewis, *Moneyball*, p. 85.

18. Lewis, *Moneyball*, p. 122.

19. Lewis, *Moneyball*, pp. 96, 99.

20. Tyler Kepner, "Astros' Luhnow Took Short Walk to New Job," *New York Times*, Dec. 17, 2011.

21. See http://www.hardballtimes.com/main/article/interview-carlos-gomez-mlb-scout/.

22. See http://www.7dvt.com/2011red-sox-baseball-scout-galen-carr.

23. Lewis, *Moneyball*, p. 128.

24. The very notion that player evaluation ever could be separated into two distinct boxes—objective and subjective—is fraught with irony. Consider Lewis's comment on p. 16 of *Moneyball*: "High school pitchers . . . were able to generate the one asset that scouts could measure: a fastball's velocity." Thus, it is implied that scouts base their evaluations largely upon a quality that can be objectively measured.

25. Lewis, *Moneyball*, p. 241.

26. The answer is exactly 100 players. Mark McGwire, with 583 career home runs but only 252 doubles, has the largest discrepancy.

27. He hit .386 on odd numbered days and .323 on even. This example is of course of no practical significance, but it illustrates the level of detail in the data.

28. Lewis, *Moneyball*, p. 88.

29. To be clear, Friedman worked for the Rays for two years before becoming their GM. During this time Sternberg had a noncontrolling interest in the team.

30. Nate Silver, *The Signal and the Noise* (New York: Penguin Press, 2012), p. 107.

31. Antonetti said as much during "Covering the Bases—An Evening with Our GMs," Mark H. McCormack Department of Sport Management at the Isenberg School of Management, UMass–Amherst, November 13, 2012.

32. For comparison, the batting table of the LahmanDB contains about 100,000 rows, so while you can't store it in Excel 2003, you can store it in Excel 2007. On the other hand, the Retrosheet events table has almost 10 million rows, rendering Excel useless.

33. Bloomberg Sports claims to have relationships with twenty-five of the thirty MLB clubs, eight to twelve of which are "enterprise clients." While exact figures are not publicly known, our information suggests that these clubs pay in the neighborhood of $100,000 per year for Bloomberg to handle their entire baseball information operation.

34. James has played a complicated role in this evolution. In *Moneyball*, he discusses the impetus for Project Scoresheet: "The lack of critical data means that "we as analysts of the game are blocked off from the basic source of information which we need to undertake an incalculable variety of investigative studies'" (p. 84). Yet James himself joined STATS, Inc. and has not played an active role in Retrosheet.

35. Chris Jaffe, "Interview: Dave 'Retrosheet' Smith," The Hardball Times, September 5, 2007. http://www.hardballtimes.com/main/article/interview-dave-retrosheet-smith/.

36. Unlike PITCHf/x, which records this data objectively through the use of high-speed cameras, STATS and BIS compile their pitch-by-pitch data from (usually multiple) human observers, who are either in the ballpark or watching the game on TV.

37. The thirty clubs nominally pay a uniform fee to MLBAM each year. However, in practice MLBAM generates several hundred millions of dollars of profit yearly, a healthy share of which is distributed to the clubs.

38. Paul DePodesta, "Mets Exec: More Data Doesn't Mean Better Data," CNBC, March 28, 2013. http://www.cnbc.com/id/100597953.

Chapter 3. An Overview of Current Sabermetric Thought I

1. Lewis, *Moneyball*, p. 124.

2. All original figures were created using the mosaic package for R. See Randall Pruim, Daniel Kaplan, and Nicholas Horton (2012). mosaic: Project MOSAIC (mosaic-web.org) Statistics and Mathematics Teaching Utilities. R package version 0.6-2. http://CRAN.R-project.org/package=mosaic. More specifically, all figures use the lattice package for graphics (Deepayan Sarkar, 2008, Lattice: Multivariate Data Visualization with R. Springer, New York) and, of course, R itself (R Core Team (2013). R: A Language

and Environment for Statistical Computing. R Foundation for Statistical Computing, Vienna, Austria, http://www.R-project.org/).

3. Strangely, NBA Houston Rockets' GM Daryl Morey is apparently responsible for both estimates. While James's model first appeared in the *1980 Baseball Abstract*, Morey estimated the value of the exponent in many other sports. See Aaron Schatz, "BackTalk: Keeping Score; Follow the Points to Find a Super Bowl Champ," *New York Times*, January 23, 2005. Morey's work on basketball showed an exponent of 13.91 and was published in *STATS Basketball Scoreboard, 1993–1994*, STATS, Inc., October 1993, p. 17.

4. Steven Miller, "A Derivation of the Pythagorean Won-Loss Formula in Baseball," *Chance Magazine* 20, no. 1 (2007), 40–48: 9698. The distribution in question is the Weibull distribution.

5. In 2002, while the A's did struggle in May, they had righted the ship by mid-June, reaching a winning percentage of .550 on May 18 and never looked back. They exceeded their expected number of wins by 3 to 6 from June 7 on.

6. Dan Fox, "Circle the Wagons: Running the Bases Part III," *Hardball Times* http://www.hardballtimes.com/main/article/circle-the-wagons-running-the-bases-part-iii/, 2005.

7. James Click, "Station to Station: The Expensive Art of Baserunning," in *Baseball Prospectus 2005*, (New York: Workman Publishing, 2005), pp. 511–519.

8. Ben Baumer and Peter Terlecky, "Improved Estimates for the Impact of Baserunning in Baseball," *JSM Proceedings*, Statistics in Sports Section, 2010.

9. See, for instance, Hirsch and Hirsch, *The Beauty of Short Hops*, passim.

10. The 67 percent is known as the R^2 or the coefficient of determination.

11. Lewis, *Moneyball*, p. 128.

12. Jim Furtado, "Introducing XR," Baseball Think Factory, 1999. http://www.baseballthinkfactory.org/btf/scholars/furtado/articles/IntroducingXR.htm.

13. There are obvious limitations to linear weights formulas, but they have proven to be effective, especially when applied to large samples. The oft-mentioned Weighted On-Base Average (wOBA) is a linear weights measure scaled to conform to typical values of OBP. For a comparison of these methods and their effectiveness, see Albert and Bennett's *Curveball*, p. 230, or Colin Wyers, "The Great Run Estimator Shootout," *Hardball Times*, April 16, 2009.

14. Lewis, *Moneyball*, p. 128.

15. For a nice primer on this issue, see Alan Schwarz, "New Baseball Statistic, With a Nod to an Old Standard," *New York Times*, February 25, 2007. Schwarz cites Victor Wang, "The OBP/SLG Ratio: What Does History Say?" *By the Numbers*, August 2008. Wang arrived at his estimate of 1.8 via trail-and-error, by finding the value x such that $x * $ OBP + SLG produced the best fit to runs scored. A mathematically precise way at estimating the value of x is to take the ratio of the coefficients of OBP and SLG from a

multiple regression model. This confirms that the optimal choice of x is about 1.84. A common misinterpretation of this result is that OBP is 1.8 times as "important" as SLG. This is not accurate, since OBP and SLG have different scales. However, we can arrive at an answer to this question by taking natural logarithms on both sides of the regression model. The ratio of the coefficients in this model is 1.5, suggesting that returns to percentage increases in OBP are 50 percent higher than returns to percentage increases in SLG.

16. Lewis, *Moneyball*, p. 128.

17. Lewis, *Moneyball*, p. 18.

18. Silver, *The Signal and the Noise*.

19. An average player's performance tends to improve up to approximately twenty-nine years of age, to level off for three years and then to begin a slow decline. Thus, we would not expect the coordinates of the dots to be identical even if batting average measured pure skill; rather, we would expect them to be close. For each player, the dots may display a temporal pattern, but this pattern would not appear in a chart of all players unless there were demographic shifts in the playing population over time.

20. A common, mathematically sensible way to model a batter's hitting ability is with a multinomial distribution. That is, identify a finite number of outcomes of a plate appearance (e.g., single, double, triple, home run, walk, hit-by-pitch, strikeout, ground out, fly out, and a catch-all category for all other outcomes) and then model each batter as having a fixed probability of ending his plate appearance with each of these outcomes. This defines a multinomial distribution, and each batter's hitting ability can be described by a vector of probabilities that sum to 1. For example, Prince Fielder singles in 13 percent of his plate appearances, doubles in 5 percent, homers in 6 percent, etc. See, for example, Brad Null, "Modeling Baseball Player Ability with a Nested Dirichlet Distribution," *Journal of Quantitative Analysis in Sports* 5, no. 2 (2009).

21. In descending order of career strikeout rate up through the 2011 season: Mark Reynolds (33.2 percent), Russell Branyan (32.9 percent), Bo Jackson (32.0 percent), Jack Cust (31.7 percent), and Rob Deer (31.2 percent). Lest we give striking out too bad a name, it does negate a potential negative—hitting into a double (or triple) play.

22. We have used other nonstandard acronyms. WK is all walks and hit-by-pitches combined, since walks and hit-by-pitches have exactly the same effect. UBB are unintentional walks. HBIP is "hits on balls in play," so the critical BABIP ratio is HBIP/BIP. The OUT circle simply captures all nonhits on balls in play, with GO and AO representing ground outs and air outs respectively.

23. Ben Baumer, "Why On-Base Percentage Is a Better Indicator of Future Performance Than Batting Average: An Algebraic Proof," *Journal of Quantitative Analysis in Sports* 4, no. 2 (2008).

24. Indeed, this was the approach taken by Tom Tango with his Marcel projection system. Marcel is notable for being very simple, relatively easy to reproduce, and fairly accurate. It is often used as a benchmark to compare more sophisticated projection systems.

25. Tom Tango, "Marcel 2012," http://www.tangotiger.net/marcel/.

26. In addition to the aforementioned work by Null, the appendix to *The Book* contains a discussion of what is essentially a Bayesian model for normally distributed variables with a normal prior distribution (Tango, Lichtman, and Dolphin, *The Book*). A more complete discussion is contained in B. B. McShane, A. Braunstein, J. Piette, and S. T. Jensen, "A Hierarchical Bayesian Variable Selection Approach to Major League Baseball Hitting Metrics," *Journal of Quantitative Analysis in Sports* 7, no. 4 (2011).

27. Leon Neyfakh, "Nate Silver Signs with Penguin in Two Book Deal Worth About $700,000," *New York Observer*, November 14, 2008. http://observer.com. Also confirmed via personal communication.

Chapter 4. An Overview of Current Sabermetric Thought II

1. Vörös McCracken, "How Much Control Do Hurlers Have?" *Baseball Prospectus*, January 23, 2001. http://www.baseballprospectus.com/article.php?articleid=878l.

2. The Cy Young Award is given to each league's best pitcher each year based on a Borda count vote by the Baseball Writers' Association of America.

3. ERA is the average number of runs a pitcher allows per nine innings that were not occasioned by an error.

4. Tyler Kepner, "Use of Statistics Helps Greinke to AL Cy Young," *New York Times*, November 17, 2009, http://www.nytimes.com/2009/11/18/sports/baseball/18pitcher.html?_r=3; Eddie Matz, "Saviormetrics," *ESPN The Magazine*, March 5, 2012, http://espn.go.com/mlb/story/_/id/7602264/oakland-brandon-mccarthy-writing-moneyball-next-chapter-reinventing-analytics-espn-magazine.

5. Lewis, *Moneyball*, p. 241.

6. That Martinez posted a .326 BABIP in 1999 (the fourteenth highest rate among the 136 pitchers with at least 500 batters faced), arguably his best season, and arguably the best season a pitcher has ever had, is truly terrifying.

7. Tom Tippett, "Can Pitchers Prevent Hits on Balls in Play," *Diamond Mind Baseball*, July 21, 2003. http://207.56.97.150/articles/ipavg2.htm. Tippett began consulting for the Red Sox around the same time, and was hired to be their director of baseball information services in 2009.

8. This argument is severely weakened by the presence of selection bias.

9. See, for example, Matt Swartz, "Ahead in the Count: Predicting BABIP," *Baseball Prospectus*, March 23, 2010. http://www.baseballprospectus.com/article.php?articleid=10333; and, Dan Rosencheck, "Hitting 'Em Where They are," Fangraphs.com, March 13, 2013. Rosencheck found that he could explain 15 percent of the variance in a pitcher's next year BABIP with the pitcher's previous year's popout rate and Z-Contact score.

10. It may be tempting to think that these results are merely the artifact of one season's worth of statistics being too small of a sample. One might also define reliability

in terms of the value of a statistic in one season and the cumulative average over the previous three years. While this does increase the reliability of BABIP a bit (e.g., the reliability for BABIP for pitchers improves from 0.17 to 0.21), it does not appreciably alter the conclusions.

11. For SIERA, see http://www.fangraphs.com/library/index.php/pitching/siera/.

12. It is not clear that SIERA is anything more than a multiple regression model with quadratic and interaction terms.

13. Lewis, *Moneyball*, p. 98.

14. See, for example, the following article from the 2009 baseball preview issue: Albert Chen, "Baseball's Next Top Models," *Sports Illustrated*, April 6, 2009, pp. 62–67.

15. Tim Marchman, "The Problems with Defensive Stats," SI.com, August 11, 2010. http://sportsillustrated.cnn.com/2010/writers/tim_marchman/08/11/marchman.defensive.stats/index.html.

16. Schwarz, *The Numbers Game*, p. 9.

17. James lamented that he "feels stupid" for not coming up with DIPS thirty years prior to McCracken's observations (Lewis, *Moneyball*, p. 240). One wonders if this comes from the fact that he invented DER to evaluate fielders, but did not think to apply the metric to pitchers.

18. The only difference is that Reached On Errors (ROE) count as outs for the purposes of BABIP, but not for DER.

19. Lewis, *Moneyball*, p. 76.

20. For a more complete survey, see Ben Baumer, Andrew Galdi, and Rob Sebastian, "A Survey of Methods for the Evaluation of Defensive Ability in Major League Baseball," JSM Proceedings, Statistics in Sports Section, 2009.

21. In fact, SAFE does not use bins at all. Rather, it fits a continuous, piece-wise smooth surface to the data.

22. Again, the methodology for obtaining that estimate varies. One can always take the simple arithmetic mean of the observations, but UZR, for example, makes corrections to account for differences in ballpark, among other factors.

23. A ball is fielded successfully if it is converted into at least one out. Thus, whether an error was made on the play is irrelevant—it is only important whether an out was recorded. This removes the subjectivity of the error designation.

24. David Appelman, "UZR Updates!" Fangraphs.com, April 21, 2010. http://www.fangraphs.com/blogs/index.php/uzr-updates/.

25. What consternation this must have caused the media, which had been touting Bay's poor UZR numbers as evidence that the Mets had been foolish in signing him to a four-year, $64 million contract in the off season. See, for example, Rob Neyer, "Upon Further Review, Bay's D not so Bad?" ESPN.com, April 30, 2010. http://espn.go.com/blog/sweetspot/post/_/id/3404/upon-further-review-bays-d-not-so-bad.

26. Dave Cameron, "Win Values Explained: Part Two," Fangraphs.com, December 29, 2008. http://www.fangraphs.com/blogs/index.php/win-values-explained-part-two/.

27. According to data downloaded from Fangraphs, 91.9 percent of the 18,847 player-position-seasons with data from 2002 to 2011 had a UZR between –5 and 5 runs.

28. Lewis, *Moneyball*, p. 136.

29. Hunter Atkins, "Rays' Joe Maddon: The King of Shifts," *New York Times*, May 7, 2012.

30. Lewis, *Moneyball*, p. 135.

31. For an interesting critique of UZR, though perhaps a bit intemperate at points, see Hirsch and Hirsch, *The Beauty of Short Hops*, pp. 80–86.

32. Lewis, *Moneyball*, p. 136.

33. In statistical terms, fielders are evaluated by the sum of the residuals between the observations and model.

34. SAFE employs a hierarchical Bayesian model. Recall the discussion of regression to the mean in the previous section on predictive analytics.

35. Hirsch and Hirsch, *The Beauty of Short Hops*, pp. 82–83.

36. Baumer, Galdi, and Sebastian, "A Survey of Methods," p. 13.

37. One potential method for attacking this problem would be to include data from many more years, but to discount it as it is further in the past.

38. Alan Schwarz, "Digital Eyes Will Chart Baseball's Unseen Skills," *New York Times*, July 9, 2009. http://www.nytimes.com/2009/07/10/sports/baseball/10cameras.html.

39. This is a natural extension of UZR, SAFE, and other models. Greg Rybarczyk proposed a similar metric called True Defensive Range (TDR) at the 2010 PITCHf/x Summit. See Rob Neyer, "FIELDf/x Is Going to Change Everything," ESPN.com, August 30, 2010. http://espn.go.com/blog/sweetspot/post/_/id/5041/fieldfx-is-going-to-change-everything.

40. Hirsch and Hirsch, *The Beauty of Short Hops*, p. 85.

41. Lewis, *Moneyball*, p. 58.

42. Lewis, *Moneyball*, p. 137.

43. The Rays' pitchers' strikeout rate was 18.6 percent in both seasons, while their walk rate declined only slightly, from 8.9 percent to 8.6 percent, and their home run rate declined from 3.1 percent to 2.7 percent.

44. The Rays' DER is .722 over that time period, with the Dodgers having the next best mark, at .714. The Rays' DER is nearly 3 standard deviations above the mean.

45. Note that this argument is independent of the question of the accuracy of defensive measurements. That is, there is a very real danger of overestimating the importance of defense because we now have the illusion of being able to measure it accurately (e.g. using UZR). However, as we have argued, there is scant evidence that the measurements made by UZR are very precise, and thus one might be tempted to argue that the importance of defense should be discounted, because the instruments for measuring it are not

precise. But the argument for the importance of defense we make above is about *team* defense, not individual fielding ability. It may very well be the case that although we are not able to measure the defensive prowess of individual fielders accurately, the effect of better team defense still plays a large role in determining the outcomes of games. Thus, it should remain an important consideration for general managers.

46. This estimate is based on Bill James's formula for expected winning percentage, which we discussed previously. The idea is that the value of the partial derivative of the function $f(rs, ra) = 162/(1 + (ra/rs)^2)$ with respect to runs scored (runs allowed) is about 0.1 (-0.1) around the point $(750, 750)$. Thus, an additional 10 runs scored (allowed) would add about 1 (-1) win to an average team's season total. While this is a convenient rule of thumb, a more careful analysis reveals that the value of these derivatives change considerably based on the run-scoring environment. For example, an additional 10 runs in the environment $(600, 900)$ would translate to only 0.725 wins.

47. Fangraphs David Wright page, http://www.fangraphs.com/statss.aspx?playerid= 3787&position=3B#value.

48. The player is 4A in the sense that he is better than a AAA player but worse than a major league player.

49. It is, however, important to remember that this is an abstraction. While such players may be plentiful, they may have significantly differing skill levels. In this sense as well, then, WAR is not a precise measurement.

50. It is useful to note that the replacement level player is significantly worse than the league-average major league player. In fact, replacement level production has no standard definition, but is usually in the range of 75-80 percent of the league average. It is also important to understand that this represents a much greater level of production than a randomly selected farmhand from A ball would likely produce, let alone your average person off the street. Some players also produce a negative value of WAR, because they perform worse than the threshold for replacement level.

51. For example, the Keeping Score column in the *New York Times* contains frequent references to WAR.

52. For a catalog of the differences between the three metrics, see http://www.base ball-reference.com/about/war_explained_comparison.shtml.

53. Dave Cameron, "Win Values Explained: Part Seven," Fangraphs.com, January 5, 2009. http://www.fangraphs.com/blogs/index.php/win-values-explained-part-seven/.

54. Among the 95,547 player-team-seasons from 1871 to 2011, nearly 82 percent had a bWAR between -1 and +1.

55. Retrosheet data is "free as in freedom." MLBAM data is only "free as in beer."

56. This would include any R, SQL, Python, or bash scripts necessary to perform the computations. It would not include any Excel procedures. This may seem inflexible, but this level of transparency is necessary for a model as complex as WAR. Also, as we have

argued previously, the sabermetric community has a long history of parallels with the open-source community that should not be discarded.

57. J. C. Bradbury, *Hot Stove Economics* (New York: Copernicus Books, 2011), pp. 92–96.

58. Of course, in practice it is considerably more complicated for a GM to sign a free agent. Such salaries are invariably guaranteed over multiyear contracts, so the issue becomes not only evaluating what the player was worth last year, but what he will be worth the coming year, and the year after next, and the year after, and so on.

59. Tango, Lichtman, and Dolphin, *The Book*.

60. Bill James, "A History of Platooning," in *The Complete Armchair Book of Baseball*, edited by John Thorn (New York: Galahad, 2004).

61. Bill James, "Underestimating the Fog," *Baseball Research Journal* 33 (2004), pp. 29–33.

62. Thomas Gilovich, Robert Vallone, and Amos Tversky, "The Hot Hand in Basketball: On the Misperception of Random Sequences," *Cognitive Psychology* 17 (1985), pp. 295–314

63. James, "Underestimating the Fog," p. 33. Nonetheless, in chapter 4 of *The Book*, Tango, Lichtman, and Dolphin find a significant clutch effect.

64. Samuel Arbesman and Steven Strogatz, "A Journey to Baseball's Alternate Universe," *New York Times,* March 30, 2008.

65. McCotter performed what statisticians call a permutation test.

66. Trent McCotter, "Hitting Streaks Don't Obey Your Rules," *Chance*, November 2011.

67. Jim Albert had written much on the subject of streakiness, and engaged McCotter in a debate about the interpretation of his work. Albert did not dispute the elegance of McCotter's method or the novelty of his findings. However, he suggested that McCotter's discovery is (1) likely the result of failing to correct for multiple testing (a smart observation that should be addressed, but is probably not enough to overturn the result); and (2) of an effect that is so small as to be of no practical significance (we find this to be less persuasive).

68. Lewis refers to this type of calculation in a passage about defense: *Moneyball*, p. 134.

69. The 119 sacrifice bunts by the Rockies were 60 percent more than the NL average in that season. Perhaps even more extreme examples were the California Angels in 1985 and 1986, who sacrificed about twice as often as the average AL team in both of those seasons.

70. Keith Woolner, "Baseball's Hilbert Problems," *Baseball Prospectus*, February 10, 2004, http://www.baseballprospectus.com/article.php?articleid=2551.

71. Email communication, September 25, 2012.

72. Ibid.

Chapter 5. The Moneyball Diaspora

1. Interestingly, cricket, where player performance is also discrete, has not witnessed a blossoming of analytics. Ahsan Butt, "Why Haven't We Seen the Moneyball-ification of Cricket?" www.firstpost.com, December 11, 2012.

2. Accordingly, a more careful modeling of the net points from a score in basketball would be a positive function to the proximity of the shot to the end of the twenty-four-second clock. This calculus changes again as a possession nears the end of a quarter in basketball.

3. For some stats, the number of occurrences might be greater outside baseball. For instance, the number of plate appearances is limited in baseball, whereas the number of shots in basketball is not as constrained. Still, some might argue that the relevant observation in baseball is the pitch, rather than the plate appearance, which would multiply the sample size several-fold.

4. For an informative history of TENDEX as well as other statistics in football, basketball, and baseball, see Dave Heeren and Pete Palmer, *Basic Ball* (Haworth, N.J.: St. Johann Press, 2011).

5. Email exchange, August 21, 2012.

6. These were players who were on the all-star team in the year of the championship or in the adjacent years.

7. APBR stands for Association for Professional Basketball Research.

8. Email from Dan Rosenbaum, August 30, 2012.

9. http://espn.go.com/nba/story/_/page/PERDiem-121214/john-hollinger-farewell -column.

10. Bob Carroll and Pete Palmer, *The Hidden Game of Football*, 1988; David Romer, "Do Firms Maximize: Evidence from Professional Football," *Journal of Political Economy* 114 (2006), pp. 340–365.

11. We are using *analytics* here basically as interchangeable with *statistical analysis* and programming. Clearly, different analysts do different types of work. For instance, it is our understanding that the Ravens hired Sandy Weil in large measure due to his skills in data management and information systems.

12. http://slashdot.org/topic/bi/buffalo-bills-latest-nfl-team-to-embrace-data-ana lytics/, accessed on January 2, 2013.

13. According to at least one observer, John Pollard, a general manager for Stats LLC, the pace of adoption of analytics in NFL front offices began to accelerate after the 2011–2012 season. See Judy Battista, "More NFL Teams Use Statisticians," *New York Times*, November 14, 2012.

14. See note 2 above.

15. See David J. Berri, Martin B. Schmidt, and Stacey L. Brook, *Wages of Wins: Taking Measure of the Many Myths in Modern Sport* (Stanford: Stanford University Press, 2006),

chs. 5-7 and David J. Berri and Martin B. Schmidt, *Stumbling on Wins: Two Economists Expose the Pitfalls on the Road to Victory in Professional Sports* (Upper Saddle River, N.J.: FT Press, 2010), chs. 2-3 and Appendix A.

16. Berri's models are log-linear.

17. Berri and Schmidt, in *Stumbling on Wins*, also report, *inter alia*, that the factors predicting when a player will be chosen in the draft do not predict how successful a player will be in the NBA and that draft position is a very weak predictor of a player's future NBA performance. See pp. 136-137.

18. In hockey, this system has proved useful, but it also has clear limitations, including the interdependency of play and the fact that role players may be advantaged or disadvantaged by it. For instance, a defender who is called upon repeatedly to go up against the top line of the opposing team is more likely to earn a minus than a defender who is up against the second line. The development of statistics for hockey analytics has been moved forward significantly by Gabriel Desjardins at behindthenet.ca.

19. According to Berri and Schmidt (*Stumbling on Wins*, p. 183), for 239 players only 7 percent of the variation in a player's adjusted plus/minus value in 2008-2009 was explained by what he did in 2007-2008. Further, if the sample is restricted to those 87 players who switched teams, the percent of variance explained falls to 1 percent.

20. Indeed, to the extent that plus/minus score provides inadequate consistency over time, a new metric based on parameters estimated in a regression that employs plus/minus as the dependent variable is likely to suffer from the same problem.

21. For an excellent discussion of the crucial role played by offensive linemen, the importance of measuring their output, and the immense complexity in doing so, see Benjamin Alamar and Keith Goldner, "The Blindside Project: Measuring the Impact of Individual Offensive Linemen," *Chance* 11 (2011), available at http://chance.amstat.org/2011/11/the-blindside-project/, and B. Alamar and J. Weinstein-Gould, "Isolating the Effect of Individual Linemen on the Passing Game in the National Football League," *Journal of Quantitative Analysis in Sports* 4, no. 2 (April 2008).

22. Passer Rating (often wrongly called "Quarterback Rating") is frequently cited during NFL game broadcasts and in the media. Its meaning is suspect for several reasons, including the use of arbitrary weights for various outcomes of passing plays and the complete exclusion of running plays.

23. See, for instance, Berri and Schmidt, *Stumbling on Wins*, appendix B, "Measuring Wins Produced in the NFL."

24. The analytical approach here is similar to that used in baseball with the run expectancy matrix. See, for one, Tom Tango et al., *The Book: Playing the Percentages in Baseball* (Dulles, Va.: Potomac Books, 2007).

25. See Jim Armstrong, "Aggressiveness Index 2011," Football Outsiders, January 27, 2012, http://footballoutsiders.com/stat-analysis/2012/aggressiveness-index-2011 for a discussion of these studies.

26. Berri and Schmidt, *Stumbling on Wins*, pp. 35–37, 182.

27. For clarity, the following statistics are the coefficient of determination (R^2), not the correlation coefficient (r).

28. Hockey stats in the NHL also show much stronger year-to-year consistency, e.g., the R^2 (percent of variance explained) for goals per minute is 63 percent.

29. Possibly compounding this effect, if your team does not have a strong winning record, then it will be hard to convince GMs around the league that you have desirable players on your roster.

30. The NBA draft lottery is an annual event held by the league in which the teams that had missed the playoffs in the previous season, or teams who hold the draft rights of another team that missed the playoffs in the previous season, participate in a lottery process to determine the order in the NBA draft. In the draft, the teams obtain the rights to amateur U.S. college players and other eligible players, including international players. The lottery winner gets the first selection in the draft. Under the current weighted lottery rules (in place since 1990), fourteen teams participate in the lottery. The lottery is weighted so that the team with the worst record, or the team that holds the draft rights of the team with the worst record, has the best chance to obtain a higher draft pick. The lottery process determines the first three picks of the draft. The rest of the first-round draft order is in reverse order of the win-loss record for the remaining teams, or the teams who originally held the lottery rights if they were traded. The lottery does not determine the draft order in the second round of the draft.

31. Graham MacAree, "Football Analytics: Finding Bill James' Cipher," www.weaint gotnohistory.com/2012/7/8/3143394/football-analytics.

32. Jere Longman,"Messi's Brilliance Transcends Numbers," *New York Times*, December 11, 2012.

33. Armstrong, "Aggressiveness Index, 2011."

34. It is interesting that even though there have been no clearly demonstrated advantages to the use of football analytics, as there have been in baseball, those NFL front offices that practice analytics treat it with the utmost confidentiality. A 2012 article in the *New York Times* commented: "Few teams like to talk about the degree to which they use analytics because they fear giving away a competitive advantage. One general manager whose team does delve into statistics, but who didn't want to be identified, wondered why the [Baltimore] Ravens announced the hire [of a director of football analytics in August 2012] at all." Battista, "More NFL Teams Use Statisticians." Meanwhile, the San Francisco 49ers have been openly stocking up with techies from Silicon Valley in anticipation of innovative applications that the techies will uncover. See Kevin Clark, "Silicon Valley Straps on Pads," *Wall Street Journal*, December 11, 2012.

35. Benjamin Alamar and Vijay Mehrotra, "Sports Analytics, Part 2," http://www .analytics-magazine.org/november-december-2011/476-sports-analytics-part-2, p. 5.

36. Battista, "More NFL Teams Use Statisticians."

Chapter 6. Analytics and the Business of Baseball

1. Although it is the received wisdom, there are detractors who question how much competitive balance or what modalities of it are the most significant. For one, see Simon Kuper and Stefan Szymanski, *Soccernomics* (New York: Nation Books, 2009). Competitive balance can apply to the uncertainty of individual games, the uncertainty of the outcome of a season, or the uncertainty of which teams will rise to the top from one year to the next.

2. To be sure, revenue sharing in MLB has other roles apart from promoting competitive balance. The way it is structured in MLB, it lowers a player's net marginal revenue product and, hence, other things being equal, lowers his salary. It is also intended to support the bottom line of financially fragile teams. For further discussion of these elements of revenue sharing, see Andrew Zimbalist, *May the Best Team Win: Baseball Economics and Public Policy* (Washington, D.C.: Brookings Institution Press, 2003).

3. It is important to clarify that we are using year-end LRD (MLB's Labor Relations Department) payroll data. LRD payroll is based on cash accounting for the entire forty-man roster. It does not use average annual contract value, as does MLB's competitive balance tax accounting. Further, it is significant that it is year-end payroll that is always more highly correlated to team win percentage than is opening day or mid-year payroll. This is because teams that are doing well generally add players (and salary) as the season progresses, and teams that are doing poorly usually dump players (and salary).

4. It is interesting to note that the R^2 between payroll and win percentage was actually higher in the years prior to the publication of *Moneyball*. For instance, between 1995 and 2002 the R^2 averaged .334. One might conjecture that this is due to the Yankees remarkable on-field success between 1996 and 2001, but this is only partially true. The R^2 only drops a few percentage points, to .274, when the Yankees are excluded from the data.

5. More precisely, the idealized standard deviation is equal to $.5/\sqrt{n}$, where .5 represents a 50 percent chance for each team to win (i.e., the assumption that talent is equally distributed across all teams) and n is the number of games played in the league per season.

6. This explanation is discussed in greater detail in Andrew Zimbalist, *Baseball and Billions* (New York: Basic Books, 1992), chapter 4.

7. Net defined local revenue basically equals local revenue minus stadium-related expenses.

8. For a more detailed discussion of these tax rates and redistribution systems, see Zimbalist, *May the Best Team Win*.

9. The age and characteristics of a team's stadium will also affect its elasticity. Other things being equal, new stadiums generate more revenue. Other factors might also be relevant, such as the team's performance the previous year, the existence of star players on the team, and the perception of the team and its owners in the community.

10. The use of team fixed effects provides for some control over differential market sizes (and branding) across teams, yielding a purer measure of the revenue response to wins at different win percentages. Similarly, the use of year fixed effects allows for the control of idiosyncratic factors in different years, such as a work stoppage or a steroid scandal. The use of the ninth degree polynomial allows for smoothing and a continuous function.

11. In his book *Diamond Dollars* (Hingham, Mass.: Maple Street Press, 2007), Vince Gennaro purports to have econometrically estimated each team's win curve, yet he provides next to no information on how he executed his empirical analysis. For instance, Gennaro apparently has done some regression analysis where revenue is the dependent variable and team wins in the current and previous years (which he apparently weighted equally) are two of the independent variables. We are not informed what the other independent variables are, nor are we told whether the relationship is tested linearly on nonlinearly, nor for what years it is tested. The issue that stands out is that there are not enough years of observation to make a statistically meaningful estimate for each team. As encountered elsewhere in the sports analytics world, Gennaro's invokes the proprietary nature of his work, presumably endowing it with some commercial value. The problem is that his methodology is a black box and cannot be vetted by scientific standards. In his case, the little he does reveal about his methodology inspires little confidence.

12. Under special circumstances, such as a new stadium, the team's fixed revenue can be modified. Such modifications, however, have had only a trivial effect on relative marginal tax rates.

13. To be more precise, each club's threshold is based on the slots of their draft picks in the first ten rounds of the amateur or Rule 4 draft, wherein each slot has a recommended signing bonus. The sum of these signing bonuses then becomes the team threshold. Since the slots are allocated in reverse order of finish in the previous year's standings, this generally means that team thresholds are in reverse order of finish. This outcome can be modified when teams lose or gain picks as a result of signing or losing free agents.

Chapter 7. Estimating the Impact of Sabermetrics

1. DER is also sometimes referred to as defensive efficiency record.

2. Both marks put Ortiz in the seventy-first percentile among the 248 major league players with at least 1,000 plate appearances between 2000 and 2002.

3. As we shall see below, from 1998 through 2002 when Dan Duquette was the Red Sox GM, the team had some of the highest saber-intensity scores over the past two decades.

4. Pedroia was described by scouts as "not physically gifted," as having a diminutive stature and loopy swing. Writing for ESPN, Keith Law, as late as 2007, opined: "Dustin Pedroia doesn't have the strength or bat speed to hit major-league pitching consistently,

and he has no power." Law went on to project the future MVP as a backup infielder. Nate Silver, *The Signal and the Noise* (New York: Penguin Press, 2012), ch. 3.

5. Silver, *The Signal and the Noise*, also relates that although his player forecasting system, PECOTA, ranked Pedroia as a top prospect, he himself gave up on Pedroia and traded him from his fantasy baseball team.

6. For example, in eXtrapolated Runs, a single is approximately 47 percent more valuable than a walk; more specifically, a single is worth .5 runs and an unintentional walk .34 runs. The relative value of a single to a walk differs slightly, but not importantly, in other linear weights models.

7. Oakland's *onbase* rating in 2002 was 1.034, which placed it in the ninety-third percentile among teams in the past twenty-seven seasons.

8. For example, computing linear weights via multiple regression on all team-seasons from 1985–2011 with at least 140 games played reveals a coefficient for sacrifice bunts that is negative (−0.0254), but not statistically significantly different from zero.

9. It is interesting to note that when we run the log of win percentage on the log of our six saber-savvy metrics, the coefficient on (the inverse of) *sacbunt* is negative (and only significant at the .10 level.) This may appear to go against the sabermetric wisdom, but it is important to keep in mind that it is only a measure of successful sacrifice bunts. If we had a measure of all the unsuccessful sacrifice bunt attempts, yielding either an unproductive out or an extra strike on the batter, then the coefficient would undoubtedly be positive.

10. Since the publication of *Moneyball*, Oakland, Seattle, and Tampa Bay appear to have put a greater emphasis on Defensive Efficiency relative to Fielding Percentage. Seattle's fascination with defense under Jack Zduriencik is well documented, as is Tampa Bay's remarkable transformation from the worst-defensive team in baseball to the best. The five leading teams in terms of *der* are as follows: Seattle (2009) 1.031; Boston (2007) 1.030; Tampa Bay (2011) 1.029; Tampa Bay (2008) 1.028; Oakland (2005) 1.027.

11. Nor is it likely that the saber-savvy GM is trying to minimize FIP relative to ERA. He is just trying to minimize FIP. To the extent that FIP is correlated with more traditional pitching measures, such as ERA, then our index will pick up some part of traditional pitching attributes and overestimate the contribution from saber-intensity.

12. As we noted in Chapter 3, sometimes ISO is defined simply as SLG − BA, in which case triples are given a higher weight than doubles.

13. More precisely, the 22 percent of players with between two and three years of major league service with the most major league service accumulated are also eligible for salary arbitration, provided that they had at least 86 days of major league service the previous year.

14. In our estimates of return to skill for individual players, the player's labor market status (reserve, arbitration eligible, or free agent) is controlled for with dummy variables for arbitration eligibility and free agency.

15. As we discuss baseball labor market inefficiencies, it is important to keep a distinction in mind. While walks or on-base percentage may have been undervalued relative to batting average from the standpoint of physical output (runs produced), it is possible that fans find base hits sufficiently more exciting to watch than walks that they are willing to pay more to see a high average hitter than a high on-base percentage hitter. If owners pick up on fan preferences and their revenue implications, then the undervaluation of OBP may be less than it seems from only assessing the impact on runs scored.

16. The regression model is explained in greater detail in the Appendix.

17. The increased value of the walk rate during the pre-*Moneyball* period (1998–2002), when power was at its apex, might seem curious. A plausible explanation is that since so many home runs were being hit during this time period, batters who managed to reach base were more likely to be driven in. Thus, the difference between being on first or second was small, since you would be driven in by a home run in either case. Conversely, if home runs were infrequent, then the value of being on second as opposed to first would be much higher. This notion coincides with the "take your walks and wait for the three-run homer" strategy attributed to Earl Weaver, but also espoused by Sandy Alderson.

18. In particular, the coefficients on OBP, ISO, DER, and FIP are all significant at the .001 level, while baserunning and sacbunts are significant at the .10 level. The equation was estimated with data from 1985 through 2011. In order to use the coefficients as weights, we take their absolute value and normalize them. The econometric details of this and other models are presented in the Appendix.

19. We normalize all the coefficients and we take the absolute value of FIP.

20. Stan Kasten, the team's president, while not an active practitioner, was an avid reader of Bill James and was well aware of the new metrics.

21. It is interesting to note that when team effects are added to this equation, the only team with a positive and statistically significant coefficient is the Oakland A's.

22. In this regression, SI is significant at the .001 level.

23. We are really estimating marginal physical product (in games) rather than WAR here. Since a replacement player produces 0 WAR by definition, the estimated values are the same.

24. Silver, *The Signal and the Noise*, p. 107, quotes Billy Beane: "The people who are coming into the game, the creativity, the intelligence—it's unparalleled right now. In ten years if I applied for this job I wouldn't even get an interview."

25. Bill Shanks's *Scout's Honor: The Bravest Way to Build a Winning Team* (New York: Sterling & Ross, 2005) is not a serious discussion of the ingredients of the team's success. It argues that the scouts were central and that the team favored high school draftees, but it provided little detail or evidence on either account.

26. Silver, *The Signal and the Noise*, p. 99.

27. Silver, *The Signal and the Noise*, p. 97.

28. Silver, *The Signal and the Noise*, p. 99. The minimum salary in 2013 is actually $490,000.

Appendix

1. The information used here was obtained free of charge from and is copyrighted by Retrosheet. Interested parties may contact Retrosheet at www.retrosheet.org.

2. Note that this definition of PAY is equivalent to team payroll divided by the MLB average payroll in that season.

3. We do not show the team fixed effects. It is interesting to note that the Oakland A's were the only team with a significant (at the .05 level) and positive coefficient. Baltimore, Detroit, the Chicago Cubs, and Kansas City all had negative and significant coefficients.

4. See http://www.seanlahman.com/baseball-archive/statistics/.

5. Although sabermetricians have corrected for ballpark effects for quite some time, there is little consensus on the most appropriate way to do so. For a fuller discussion see Carl Morris et al., "Improving Major League Baseball Park Factor Estimates," *Journal of Quantitative Analysis in Sports* 4, no. 2(April 2008).

6. Of course, this is guaranteed by the least squares fitting procedure used in the payroll model.

7. J. K. Hakes and R. D. Sauer, "An Economic Evaluation of the Moneyball Hypothesis," *Journal of Economics Perspectives* 20, no. 3 (2006), pp. 173–185. Also see, J. K. Hakes and R. D. Sauer, "The Moneyball Anomaly and Payroll Efficiency: A Further Investigation," *International Journal of Sport Finance* 2, no. 4 (November 2007), pp. 177–189.

INDEX

ACKNOWLEDGMENTS

Many practitioners, colleagues, friends, and sports industry mavens have been enormously helpful to us in the preparation of this book. In particular, we would like to thank Ben Alamar, Jim Albert, Sandy Alderson, Dave Allen, TJ Barra, Dave Berri, Roger Blair, Dave Cameron, Will Carroll, James Click, Daniel Cohen, Mark Cuban, Frank Deford, Christina DePasquale, Paul DePodesta, Dan Duquette, Meaghan Fileti, Adam Fisher, Sarah Gelles, Jessica Gelman, Gary Gillette, Wyc Grousbeck, Dave Heeren, John Henry, Nick Horton, Bill James, Shane Jensen, Michael Kalt, Ari Kaplan, Stan Kasten, Ken Kovash, Jonathan Kraft, Keith Law, Randy Levine, Mickey Lichtman, Chris Long, Larry Lucchino, Rob Manfred, Chris Marinak, Trent McCotter, Daryl Morey, Dan Okrent, Dean Oliver, Pete Palmer, Chris Picardo, James Piette, John Ricco, Dan Rosenbaum, Dan Rosencheck, Ken Rosenthal, Steve Ross, Skip Sauer, Alan Schwarz, Mark Shapiro, Nate Silver, Mark Simon, Dave Smith, Stacey Solliday, Charles Steinberg, John Thorn, Tom Tippett, Tom Verducci, Earl Weaver, and Frank Westhoff. We are especially grateful to Jim Logue and Tom Tango, who provided careful comments on our entire manuscript.

More generally, we would like to thank all those in the sports industry who have unselfishly shared their time, expertise, anecdotes, and passion with us over the years.

We would also like to lovingly thank our families, Cory, Maggie, Don, Polly, Jeanne, Shelley, Alex, Ella, Jeff and Mike, for supporting us through our distractions and preoccupations while working on this project.